HOW TO PRESS
AMERICA'S
RESET BUTTON

A simple, safe, legal and effective method
to regain control of our government

SEAN BURKE

VIAVERA
BOOKS

Published by:

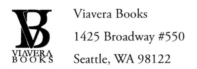

Viavera Books
1425 Broadway #550
Seattle, WA 98122

Printed in the United States

Special discounts are available on quantity purchases by corporations, associations, churches, schools, and others. For details, contact the publisher at the address above or email info@viaverabooks.com.

ISBN 978-0-99697-760-9

10 9 8 7 6 5 4 3 2 1

Cover design by Mike Falkow
Illustrations by Sean Burke

For my children and the future generations
of Americans who will inherit the country
we leave them.

contents

A Note From the Author.................vii

Introduction: A Simple Solution......xi

Who Am I to Write this Book?.........xiii

What Are We Talking About?...........xxi

Warnings & Notes...........................xxvii

CHAPTER 1   You're Not Alone.....................................1

CHAPTER 2   A New View...5

CHAPTER 3   What's Going On Down There?...............11

CHAPTER 4   Let the Games Begin...............................17

CHAPTER 5   The Test...27

CHAPTER 6   The Unshakable Truth............................37

CHAPTER 7   Truth & Lies..43

CHAPTER 8   We, the Group Called Americans............51

CHAPTER 9   The Duties of a Board............................63

CHAPTER 10   Purpose..69

CHAPTER 11   Management...77

CHAPTER 12   Is It or Isn't It?...................................83

CHAPTER 13   What's the Problem with a Little Debt?...97

CHAPTER 14   We Are Them, They Are Us....................105

CHAPTER 15   Broken System...........................111

CHAPTER 16   The Hidden War.........................123

CHAPTER 17   Fragile Future...........................129

CHAPTER 18   No News Doesn't Mean Good News......139

CHAPTER 19   Not My Problem........................143

CHAPTER 20   We the People...........................149

CHAPTER 21   Management Qualifications..................155

CHAPTER 22   Our Power.............................165

CHAPTER 23   Together...............................173

CHAPTER 24   After Reset............................179

CHAPTER 25   National Security.......................185

CHAPTER 26   Our Children's Country.................191

CHAPTER 27   Your Reason to Reset...................197

CHAPTER 28   Share................................201

For More Information.......................205

Appendix...............................207

Bibliography.............................213

A Note From the Author

THIS BOOK IS THE RESULT OF MY PERSONAL journey to save our country after suddenly realizing a couple of years ago that, like a ship headed relentlessly toward rocky cliffs, our country was headed unchecked toward destruction. It was clear to me that unless I was somehow able to alter its course for the better, my children and their children would not enjoy the level of American freedom and prosperity that I've enjoyed throughout my life. I admit that my quest was bold and possibly delusional, believing that one person could make real change to our massive government, but I didn't feel I had any other choice—I simply felt I needed to urgently do something.

After extensive research, I found a way that we can take back control of our country and significantly shake up the political status quo in Washington D.C. I found a way that we can change the direction in which our country is heading. I found a way that we can make real, lasting and incredibly substantial change. In the end, what I discovered was our country's reset button.

When I began this journey, I was looking for a way that I could personally bring about change, but ended up with a way that we *all* can, if we work together.

My goal is to walk you down the path I took to discover our country's reset button so that hopefully you can see it as I do.

The idea I propose in this book is entirely legal, non-violent, simple, fast and enormously powerful. It's entirely new. It's not slanted toward any political party or idealism. It doesn't attack the president, nor does it tear apart Congress. It doesn't drum on only the negative and proclaim that all is lost. Rather, it presents a simple, easy way that we can oversee our government practically and ensure that it continually performs to our liking.

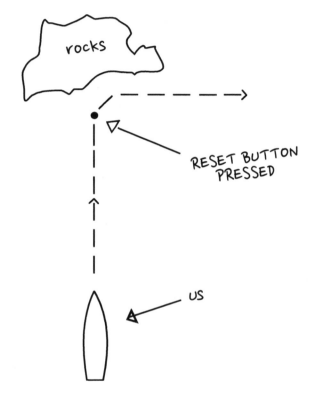

This book was not written to be read and debated by scholars. It was written specifically for U.S. citizens who are frustrated with the direction their country is heading in, and who feel their government has lost sight of its duty to them. It was written for those who want to have a voice in how their country is run.

This book is different in that it doesn't just talk about the problems our country is facing, but actually offers a real, practical way for us to regain control over our government. It wasn't written just to be debated or studied; it was written for *application*.

The idea of fixing our government isn't new. Thousands of organizations exist today with this as their goal. Some work toward amending the Constitution, some suggest making government smaller, and others think the government should provide more services for us all. Then there are the groups that feel an armed overthrow of our government is the only way to make a change. On top of all this are the millions of Americans who think (and worry) about this problem every day. A great deal of human energy and thought is spent on this one goal—and for good reason, since there is an enormous amount of concern about where our country is heading, and the condition it will be in for our children and those who come after us. Many of the solutions proposed by individuals and groups are very good and valid, and our government may very well be better with them implemented. The solution presented here doesn't invalidate those ideas in any way, but rather will make it easier for the best and most important of those solutions to be put into action.

If we all follow the idea outlined in this book, we'll return the control of our government to the only source of its power, which is *us*. And once we've regained that control, we'll make some simple changes to how our government operates, to ensure that it doesn't just go back to business as usual.

In order to fix our government, we need ideas and innovation and participation and interest from all of us. But the good news is it *can* be done, non-violently and with relative ease.

By turning to the next page, you are embarking on the same journey of discovery I took—some of it earlier in my life, some of it more recent, but discoveries just the same—to recognize the power we hold and the change to our government that we can truly and easily bring about.

Like any good journey, this one may present a few challenges to overcome. Any traditional, longstanding views of our government, and the various forces at work to control it, may be challenged by some of the ideas and perspectives presented herein. But fear not— your ideas and point of view are yours to keep or change as you wish, for only you can decide what's true for you. I only hope that you'll give the ideas I present here a chance, and that you'll persevere through to the final pages—to the end of the journey—so you too can discover how you can help save our country.

INTRODUCTION

A simple solution

THROUGHOUT OUR COUNTRY'S HISTORY, THERE have been periods of both prosperity and struggle.

We've been through wars, some small and some long and costly, both in terms of economic outlay and loss of human life. We've survived many trials.

We were the first to land on the moon.

Our military is currently still the mightiest.

Our economy is twice the size of any other country in the world. Most would agree that we're still the most powerful.

But we've also seen our share of troubles, and over the years Americans haven't been shy about voicing their disagreement. In 1963, over 200,000 people gathered in Washington D.C. in support of the movement to improve civil rights for black people. In 1969, half a million people gathered in the same city to protest our country's involvement in the Vietnam War. These protests were successful in raising awareness for very specific points of citizen disagreement.

But what do we do if we simply disagree with the *overall* direction of our country? Should we take to the streets and march, holding signs that read "Down With Washington"? Would that bring about the change we want? Or should we work to overthrow our government by taking up arms and storming the White House? Would that solve anything?

Just a few years ago, large numbers of people camped out in various cities around the country to protest social and economic inequality in what was called the Occupy movement. It generated a tremendous amount of media coverage and debate. It clearly communicated that there was a segment of our society that was unhappy. Did all the energy, work, emotion and hope expended by those who participated create any effective change? Did it improve decision-making in Congress? Did all that effort actually cause any lasting change to the conditions being protested? Unfortunately, from what I can tell, it did not.

Does that mean change isn't possible? Should we just quit trying? Is it all hopeless? Though sometimes it may certainly feel that way, and many—possibly even you—may have given up, it's not hopeless. We *can* make a change.

The solution lies in taking action that's simple, can be done easily by any who choose to do it and will make *real*, *sweeping* and *tangible* change.

And is there such a solution? I'm here to tell you there *is*. I looked for it, and I found it: a simple, powerful reset button firmly embedded in our government by our Constitution. It's been operational since our country was formed, but I'm not sure it's ever been fully pressed. Wary of a government that would lose its way, grow too powerful and fail to accomplish the purposes set out for it, those who wrote our Constitution put it in place. They wisely—and boldly—installed it in our government to be easily and quickly pressed by any citizen who felt that a dramatic change in their government was needed.

But me finding and pressing this reset button does us little good unless you discover it and press it, too. You see, our country's reset button is powerful, but only as powerful as the number of people who press it. We need millions to find it and press it with us.

I found the reset button, and it was hidden in plain view. Once you see it for yourself, only you can decide whether to press it or not.

I hope you will—if not for you or me, then for those Americans who will come after us and have to live with the negative ramifications of our government's actions, if they're left unchanged.

who Am I to write this Book?

I T'S A GREAT QUESTION, AND ONE THAT SHOULD be asked.

I'm not a lawyer or professor or billionaire. I don't work for the government, a D.C. lobby group or scholarly think tank. I've never been elected to office and have no plans to run.

I'm an American, born and raised in the Upper Midwest in a small idyllic town on a beautiful winding river. I spent my summers as a youth swimming, water skiing and generally enjoying the wide-open country that was always near.

The little town I grew up in was unique in that it was our state's capital. And one of the great benefits of living in a small community was that we knew most everyone, from the postman to the governor. After school, my friends and I would sometimes play in the capitol building, exploring the various rooms and passageways, and generally had the run of the place.

One of my parents' friends was a farmer who ran for Congress. At a very early age, I spent hours helping his campaign by stuffing letters into envelopes for a mailing before an election. He won that election and spent many terms in Congress before he ran for the U.S. Senate and won. At that point, I was in college and spent one of my summer breaks working as an intern in his office in Washington D.C.

What many people don't know is that the majority of the people actually doing the day in, day out work in the D.C. congressional offices are around twenty-four years old.[1] For many of them, working on the staff of a senator or congressperson is their first job. And these young people are given huge responsibilities. As a twenty-one-year-old intern, I was a good example of this. I was asked to look into newspaper reports suggesting that there were problems in a nationwide network of banks overseen by Congress that supplied loans to farmers, ranchers and others with homes and businesses in the rural areas of America. This network of banks I'm referring to is called the Farm Credit System (FCS). Today, it ranks in size as one of the top ten banks in the U.S.

My job was to see if there was any truth to those newspaper reports. Over a period of a couple weeks, I made calls to everyone quoted in the press regarding problems with the FCS. Besides this being important work, it was also fun. How often do you get to call someone on behalf of a U.S. senator? In the end, every person I spoke to in the FCS said there were no problems, everything was in order and all was good. And so, of course, I passed that information—with the details of who said what—on to the senator. He was relieved.

A month after I had completed my internship and headed back to college, the FCS crashed and the agricultural industry in the U.S. experienced a debilitating recession. The government agency that oversees the FCS estimated that 200,000 to 300,000 farmers were on the brink of bankruptcy. The FCS lost $2.7 billion that year, the largest loss by any bank up to that point in U.S. history.[2] For the farm sector, it felt like the return of the Great Depression. Very quickly, Congress passed legislation to provide additional funding to the FCS so the network of banks could avoid collapse.

And what about those FCS executives who had assured me all was well just a few weeks before? They were now quoted in the press saying that the problems had been coming on for a long time. This

---

[1] Rosiak, "Congressional Staffers, Public Shortchanged by High Turnover, Low Pay."

[2] Farm Credit Administration, "History of FCA and the FCS."

shocked me. Many of them hadn't had the courage to tell me—to tell Congress—that a massive downturn was coming. They lied. I learned that what one sees on the surface isn't always the way it really is.

After graduating from college with a degree in business, I worked in entry-level positions in a number of businesses before moving to Los Angeles and finding work in the entertainment industry, which I've now worked in for over twenty-five years. Fortunately, one of my positions entailed traveling extensively around the U.S. and other countries. In all, I've traveled to twenty-three countries and have set foot on every continent on earth but Antarctica.

For many years, I've been researching and thinking of various ways to help bring about real change in our government. But how can one person really make any change? How can one person do something that actually might positively affect the future of our nation? It's a puzzle I've been trying to solve for decades.

One area I've long been determined to change is the flow of money to our elected officials from organizations and individuals by way of lobbyists. I think few people really understand the influence of the lobby industry in Washington. I feel that, if they did, they would be appalled. So how do you educate the entire country on the truth about the lobby industry? Well, I decided to develop a dramatic TV show in the vein of *The West Wing* that told true stories about lobbyists and the tactics they employ. I firmly believe that information—*factual* information—is vital to any population in order to make the best decisions for their country. I thought that if the show became successful and enough people watched it over an extended period of time, they would have a better understanding of what really goes on in D.C. and take some action to cause much-needed reform.

Over the next couple of years I developed the concept further, wrote the first episode and plotted out the first two seasons with another writer. It was going to be great. Epic, in fact. Certain to win Emmy Awards. The topics we could explore on the show were endless. The reality of sex and drugs in the lobby industry would play right into a great drama on HBO, Showtime or Netflix.

With the help of many friends well-connected in the entertainment industry, we took the idea around and pitched it to various studios and production companies. The highlight for me was pitching the show to Peter Roth, the Warner Bros. TV executive who had said yes to *The West Wing* and had guided it to becoming an award-winning show.

In the end, we actually came close to getting the show made. The pinnacle was when a TV producer took the concept of my show to Ron Howard's TV company, which then signed on as the show's producer with Fox TV agreeing to finance it. A well-known TV star signed on as the lead. The idea was finally presented to the president of ABC who, unfortunately, didn't feel it was a show for his network. In the end, many liked the idea, including Showtime, which gave it a very positive review. But it was never made and still sits on my computer, ready to leap into action. The show is titled *DC Lobby*.

Shortly thereafter, I founded a non-profit organization dedicated to privacy rights for individuals. This emerged from my experience overseeing security for celebrities—one of many roles throughout my career in the entertainment industry. I also held the position as the primary bodyguard for a few of my celebrity clients, and it was in this role that I experienced up close and personal the invasive, abusive and aggressive antics of the paparazzi. Before I was involved in security, the paparazzi didn't mean much to me. And initially, when I began interfacing with them as my clients traveled around, I thought they were pretty harmless. But over time, my point of view changed as I witnessed them doing anything to get a photo, from taunting, harassing behavior to breaking laws. It finally got to a point where I could no longer tolerate it. I consider a person's right to privacy as something fundamental that shouldn't need to be granted by any government, but something that innately belongs to all humans.

After watching the paparazzi get more and more aggressive,

dangerous and intrusive, I formed a non-profit corporation called the Paparazzi Reform Initiative. I traveled to the capitol of California in Sacramento and spoke in front of various committees and, that year, we were successful in getting a new law passed by the legislature and signed into law by Governor Schwarzenegger.

That's me with the Speaker
of the California Assembly

From there, it grew. Since I founded the organization six years ago, we've helped get four new laws on the books in California. But more importantly to me, we've helped educate millions of people on the issue through our website and interviews with the press, including the *Los Angeles Times*, the *Wall Street Journal*, *The Today Show* and many more.

The results on the street have been positive. The Beverly Hills Police Department reported a sixty-nine percent drop in paparazzi-related incidents in their city between 2008 and 2011.[3]

I've learned a lot through all of this, the most important lesson being that it's possible to make positive change if done thoughtfully and intelligently. I've come to firmly believe that it's always possible to do *something* to improve negative conditions or situations in life. When I started my mission to improve the privacy rights of those harassed by the paparazzi, I was just one person with an idea facing a powerful, decades-old (and well-funded) force. I truly had no idea how it would turn out, but knew I couldn't *not* try to do something about it.

It was in this frame of mind that I turned my attention a couple of years ago to my growing concern about the health and longevity of our country. The Great Recession of 2008-2009 had come and gone, and it appeared as though the country was recovering. The federal budget deficits were higher than at any other time in history (an understatement), and Congress was fractured and its members were battling each other. The credit rating for our country was downgraded as our national debt skyrocketed. Congress was so dysfunctional that it almost allowed our government to default on our debt, which would have resulted in a potentially catastrophic economic crisis around the globe.

I finally got to a point where I couldn't sit back any longer. I felt that I couldn't stay quiet and assume that it was all going to be okay and that "they" were going to somehow guide us down the right path. I had lost confidence in our government leaders, as well as my belief that they were working in my best interest. I became very worried about what the country would be like for my children and their children if it kept on the same path. Various ideas and solutions came to mind about what I could do to help. But after researching them more, each one subsequently failed to offer real change.

---

[3] City of Beverly Hills Study Session Action Minutes, point 9.

And then, late last year, the idea of pushing America's reset button came to me.

This book is my attempt to guide you down the path to not only seeing the button for yourself, but hopefully compelling you to join me in pressing it.

That's my story. That's who I am, and why I've written this book. It's been my lifelong pursuit to do all I can to help improve the world around me, as best I'm able. And my concern for our country, and the shape it will be in for our children, has led me here. I found America's reset button, and now it's my job to show it to you so you might press it yourself.

What Are We Talking About?

Before we get started, it's important to understand what we're talking about. In truth, it's here that I started my journey—digging in and making sure I fully understood some of the basic terms used to describe our country and government.

How important do you think it is for a doctor to fully understand all the words in the material he studied to earn his degree? Or the pilot flying the next plane you board? What might occur if they have incorrect information? This can be extended out to a frightening degree. For example, what if our president and elected leaders were operating off of incorrect information? What would the results of their actions be? It certainly wouldn't be good for us!

Since I was looking for correct answers that might fix the many problems I felt were being caused by our government, I knew I needed to review some of the basic words regarding our government to make sure I had clarity on the subject.

But there was a danger here that I needed to be aware of: thinking I knew the meaning of a word or term when I really didn't. This can easily happen with words that we hear or read often—we assign some meaning to them that may be incorrect, or only partially correct.

To make matters worse, it can also be difficult to know whether information we read and hear about our government is true. Virtually everyone has an opinion, and they are rarely based on facts. And then there are the various people, groups, corporations and foreign governments that try to persuade us all to think a certain way regarding a candidate, our economy, foreign policy or another aspect of our government. This stream of information comes at us from the TV, newspapers, friends, co-workers, employers, Facebook, the Internet, etc. It's extremely difficult to find unbiased information about what is factually going right or wrong in D.C. It's no wonder things can seem confusing and complex sometimes.

This is even more reason to ignore what people say for a minute and look for yourself at the foundation of what we're talking about. Even if you think you know what all these terms mean, it never hurts to be reminded of their meanings again, especially when things are looking over-complicated.

GOVERNMENT: That organization made up of individuals that handles the various aspects of our country—defense, international affairs, education, roads, tax collection, law enforcement, creating new laws, criminal prosecution, etc. The word "government" comes from a Greek word meaning "to steer."[1] In its most basic, simplest form, the government is simply steering.

POLITICS: A word we hear all the time and probably associate with those things called "politicians." The word simply means "having to do with the government."[2] It comes from a Greek word that means "citizen."[3] When you connect the root of "politics" to the root of "government," you get "citizen steering."

CONSTITUTION: Comes from a Latin word that means "establish."[4] A constitution is a written document outlining the basic

---

[1] Oxford English Dictionary.

[2] Collins English Dictionary.

[3] Merriam-Webster Dictionary.

[4] Oxford English Dictionary.

rules, ideas, laws, powers and restrictions of a group or government. In the U.S., it's the foundation of our government. It protects our freedom of speech and religion, establishes our three branches of government, declares who is eligible to vote and defines many other guidelines. It is the foundational law of our country.

The principles set out in that document are what we fought Great Britain for in the Revolutionary War. And even after we'd won, some people were still inclined to have a king or queen rule the U.S. But John Adams, Thomas Jefferson, James Madison and others wrote articles and booklets to inform and convince the people living in the colonies to vote in favor of the new Constitution and new form of government, which established our country as a republic, not a monarchy. Nine out of the thirteen colonies needed to approve the Constitution for it to take effect (in the end, they all approved it).

It's ultimately in our best interest, as well as that of our children and their children, to keep a close watch and ensure that our government follows and doesn't violate the very document that established it.

The Constitution grants us freedoms that the citizens of many other countries don't enjoy. It's up to us to be watchful and insist that those freedoms don't get taken away, or allow them to fade from use.

DEMOCRACY: Many people think that our form of government is a democracy, but it isn't. In fact, the word "democracy" isn't even mentioned in our Constitution. The definition of true democracy is "rule by the majority," meaning whatever the majority decides is law.

The word "democracy" comes from a Greek word meaning "the people rule."[5] For example, if a town were operating as a true democracy, every citizen would be able to vote on *every* decision

---

[5] Ibid.

the town made. As an extreme scenario to demonstrate how a true democracy would work, the people in a town practicing democracy could come together to decide whether a person should be killed or not. If the majority voted in favor of the killing, it could legally be carried out, regardless of whether the person was guilty of *anything*. In another example, if the majority decided that a minority group couldn't own property, then that restriction could become law. A historical example of democracy in action occurred around 400 BC in Athens, Greece, when the city had a rule in place that anyone could be removed and barred from it for a period of ten years if the majority of citizens voted in favor of it. By the vote of the majority, the decision effectively became law, and many people were banished through this process.[6]

The U.S. is commonly thought of as a democracy, since each citizen has a vote, but the more accurate term for our form of government is "republic."

REPUBLIC: In a republic, like a democracy, the citizens are in charge. The primary difference is that, in a republic, the citizens elect representatives to run the government *for* them, so they can continue on with their lives and don't have to be directly involved in every decision. Instead of a having a king or queen, a republic usually has an elected leader, like a president.

To refine this even further, the United States is a "constitutional republic," meaning we have a constitution that sets the general *guidelines* for how the government is to be conducted. The word "republic" comes from a Latin phrase that means "entity of the people."[7] Of all the terms we need to review, this one is key—it tells us what our form of government is, and the principle our country

---

[6] Encyclopedia Britannica, "Ostracism."

[7] Oxford English Dictionary.

is based on. Understanding this is vital to understanding how we might improve or fix our country. The most important point is that *we*, the *citizens*, hold the power over our government, based on our Constitution. And the specific power that we have is to elect *representatives*. We are granted supreme power by the Constitution and are senior in importance to our representatives, not the other way around.

And to refine this just a bit more, the eligible voters are the ones who have this power. An "eligible voter" for national elections is someone who is at least eighteen years old, is a citizen and meets a few other guidelines that tend to vary from state to state. The eligible voters are in charge of our country. Let me repeat that: no matter what anyone else says or does, and no matter how it might appear, the *eligible voters* are in charge of the United States. We don't have to ask for permission, or feel shy about it—*we* are the keepers of our country and the government that runs it, and we must fulfill this role we have.

As Benjamin Franklin was leaving the room where the final form of our Constitution had been decided upon, a woman asked him if our country would be a republic or monarchy. His answer was very telling: "A republic, if you can keep it."[8]

DEBT vs. DEFICIT: These two words are used so much in the media when referring to our country's financial health that it's easy to lose track of what they really mean. The word "debt" of course means "an amount which is owed." "Deficit" or "budget deficit" simply means the amount that our government needs to *borrow* in order to pay for everything in our national budget. It's the amount of money needed that the government doesn't have. A deficit *increases* our country's debt.

---

[8] Bartleby, "Respectfully Quoted: A Dictionary of Quotations. 1989."

For you and me, a budget deficit means either making more money, cutting back on our spending or going into debt. For our government, it almost always simply means taking on more debt, which is why we're currently $18 trillion in debt.[9] Our government leaders like to brag about "cutting the deficit." They promote this as a good thing, and in general it is, but just because our deficit is less isn't cause for celebration; it means we still have to *borrow* money to pay all our bills. Having any amount of deficit means our debt continues to *grow*. What our government should be excitedly announcing to the media is when our government will have a budget *surplus*, which would mean we could actually pay down some of our debt. To you and me, it would mean we'd have some money left over to pay down debts, put in savings or invest. That would be something to get excited about.

These are some of the key terms to understand as we move forward, but don't hesitate to look up any other terms you aren't certain of that I might use in the book as you read along, or that you run into when reading or listening to the media. The only way we're going to develop an effective strategy for fixing our country is by accurately *understanding* the information we need to process.

---

[9] Treasury Direct, "The Debt to the Penny and Who Holds It."

warnings & Notes

I THINK IT'S ONLY FAIR TO GIVE YOU A FEW warnings and notes before you go any further:

1. This book is dangerous to those who want to control our country for their own purposes. They won't want you reading it. They won't like the ideas in it. They won't want you carrying these ideas out.

2. The idea of taking back control of our country is not new and has been attempted (with varying degrees of success) a number of times since we left Great Britain. But what *is* new is the method described in this book of how to change our government without a drop of bloodshed, violence, sweat or anything illegal. In fact, the method is so simple that it can be overlooked by mistake.

3. It's highly probable that the "experts" will say pressing America's reset button would never work or would cause more damage than good. These will most likely be the same experts who haven't been able to fix our government despite their own ideas and attempts. There is no doubt that if we follow the ideas outlined in this book, the country will change dramatically for the better. But that, of course, is for you to decide—read on and see what you think.

4. I am not a political expert, economist, lawyer, TV commentator or college professor. This book wasn't funded by a political party. I'm

not secretly backed by a major corporation or a billionaire pushing a particular ideology or philosophy.

5. Unlike many of the ideas that get pushed around about our government, this idea has no hidden agenda.

6. Unless we *do* something new, *nothing* will change. But change takes action outside of "normal" action. Change takes some disagreement, sometimes a little courage, definitely some forward thinking and a bit of faith. Ultimately, we can *hope* that others are taking care of things, or we can *act* in a way that makes things go the way *we* want them to. And in answer to all those discouraging thoughts that might flood your mind when you consider making any kind of substantial change to your government: you are much more powerful than you believe, and if you use that power correctly and accurately, substantial change can and will happen to our government.

7. While reading this book, you might just rehabilitate some of your lost hope in our country. You might actually start thinking you *can* do something to make change. If that does happen, don't say I didn't warn you.

Okay, here we go, and may our country never be the same.

CHAPTER 1

You're Not Alone

ARE YOU CONCERNED ABOUT WHAT THE country will be like when your children are grown and living their lives? Are you disappointed in the party you belong to or, for that matter, any of the parties? Do you think Congress is doing a poor job?

Have you gotten to the point where you feel that there's nothing you can do to fix your government? Have you given up? Have you quit participating?

If you answered yes to any of these questions, rest assured that you're not alone.

About half the voters surveyed after the 2014 midterm election felt that the next generation wouldn't enjoy a better life than we have today.[1] More than fifty percent of those surveyed expressed negative feelings toward both the Democratic and Republican parties.[2]

Out of those who could have voted in the 2014 midterm election, 140 million *didn't*—the lowest voter turnout in a national election in seventy years.[3]

The mayor of Los Angeles—a city of 3.8 million people—was elected by just 220,000 Angelinos in 2013.[4]

Only forty percent of the voters showed up to elect a new mayor of Chicago in 2011.[5]

---

[1] Calmes and Thee-Brenan, "Surveys of Voters Signal Dismay With Both Parties."

[2] Rasmussen Reports, "53% Think Neither Political Party Represents the American People."

[3] United States Election Project, "2014 November General Election Turnout Rates."

[4] Welsh, "L.A. Mayoral Runoff Another Low Mark in Voter Turnout: 23.3%.

[5] CBS News Chicago, "Chicago Voter Registration at Record Low."

Just thirteen percent of likely voters rate Congress's performance as good or excellent.[6]

Three million New Yorkers skipped voting for their new mayor in 2013.[7]

Sixty-five percent of us feel that our country is headed down the wrong track.[8]

In 2011, ten changes to the Texas Constitution were put forth to be decided by the citizens of Texas. Only nine percent of those who could have voted actually did. Twelve million people did not.[9]

It has gotten so bad that the city of Los Angeles has seriously considered giving people a chance to win a cash prize if they vote.[10]

The problem is this: If we quit, who controls our country?

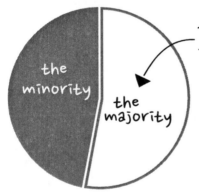

Source: Data from Rasmussen Reports (2014).

[6] Rasmussen Reports, "Congressional Performance."

[7] Janison, "Voter Turnout Disappointing in Tuesday's Elections."

[8] Rasmussen Reports, "Right Direction or Wrong Track."

[9] Texas Secretary of State, "Turnout and Voter Registration Figures (1970–Current)."

[10] Zahniser, "Panel Wants L.A. to Look at Using Prizes to Boost Voter Turnout."

———————————————

"Nobody will ever deprive the American people of the right to vote except the American people themselves and the only way they could do this is by not voting."

—President Franklin Roosevelt during a radio message on October 5, 1944

———————————————

CHAPTER 2

A New View

THE FIRST THING WE NEED TO DO ON THIS
journey to finding the reset button is take a giant step back from our
day-to-day lives and try to get a better perspective of where we are and
what's going on around us in our country.

In this chapter, you're going to need to use a bit of imagination to
get the proper view of things. When you were younger—or maybe
just yesterday—you may have daydreamed and left the realities of the
world around you for a moment and entered another world. Maybe
you traveled mentally to Italy, or found yourself talking to an old friend
or remembered something funny one of your children said to you
earlier in the day. This is a capacity we all have within us, to imagine
and visualize things.

Ready to begin? This exercise may seem a bit unusual at first, but
bear with me—there's a point to it, I promise.

While on earth, we can see what everyone else sees: trees, homes,
businesses, other people, etc. Each of us sees and experiences the
world in which we live. We each have our everyday routines, our own
perspectives, our friends and loved ones, our joys and our worries—
our own worlds in which we live, love and work. This is our personal
sphere. For some of us, it might be huge and vast and encompass a lot
of territory and many people—as it might be for, say, an airline pilot.
Or it might encompass a very small amount of space and only one or
two other people—as it might be for someone in their older years who
spends most of their time at home.

Whatever your sphere or territory, even if you're the president of our country, in order to take this journey to find our country's reset button, you need to get to a certain point—and this is something you can easily do with a little imagination—above and outside your normal sphere to get a better glimpse of where you are and how things work.

Imagine an astronaut who climbs into a capsule and is rocketed away from the sphere she's accustomed to in her life. As she looks down, she can see her town becoming a speck in the mass of land that is her state, and then that state becoming a small piece within the landmass of the country. As her capsule orbits the earth, she can see that not all the world is in winter, as her area is, but that the southern part of the planet is green and enjoying summer. She can see very clearly that the landmass of her country floats separately in a giant sea of water that encircles the world, which clearly separates Europe and Asia from its shores.

This is the same perspective you need to achieve regarding our country. Through your imagination, take a giant step back from the day in, day out world in which you live, and get a similar look at our country as what that astronaut saw. Just mentally expand your look a bit to take in the concept of our entire country in one look or thought. There isn't a right way or wrong way to do this—it will be unique to each of us, since we're all completely unique and individual.

It's important to take this step back from our own individual worlds and disconnect a bit, because we need to take a good look at what's going on in our country on a much broader scale. Every now and again, as one is traveling along a certain path on the way to somewhere, it's smart to get to a high spot and look ahead at what weather, terrain and distance lie ahead, and to make sure the course being followed is the correct one.

This exterior perspective is going to be important to maintain, or return to, as you move through these pages. And when you step back from your daily life, hopefully you will also be able to leave behind some of your points of view about our government. What I offer here in these pages might be a new and different look at our government and those who run it and how we might go about fixing it. Remember that, in the end, whether you accept or reject what I offer here is entirely up to you, and whether you decide to actually push the reset button once you see it—if you see it—will be entirely your choice. Only you can decide what to believe, so it's okay to loosen your grip a bit on your opinions and ideas about our government, how it must or shouldn't operate, what terrible or wonderful things it's doing for us all and how those with opposing views to yours are bad, evil, misguided or just plain stupid. It's okay to loosen your grip on all of this. When you're reading these pages, give yourself a chance to see another point of view about our government.

MIND FULL   WITH ROOM

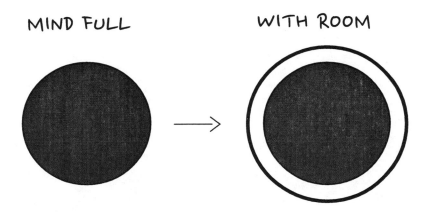

So, are you game to give this a go? Are you willing to take a step back and take a broader, maybe fresher look at our government?

If your answer is yes, then please do that now. Step back and get that bigger picture. Get the concept of our entire country and the 300 million other American citizens out there, working and living their lives. Get the concept of our elected leaders in Washington striving—whether correctly or not—to pass laws and guide our country into the future. And get a feel for the pressures pushing against them that help shape their decisions, whether from friends or family, those who elected them, corporations, non-profits, foreign governments or even their own fears and desires. And take a moment to realize that those elected officials are human and that they have families, they need to pay bills like the rest of us, they worry about their significant others just like we do and they're citizens—American citizens—just like we are.

With your 200-mile-high view of our country, bordered on both sides by water, couldn't we easily liken it to a ship? This is an analogy I'll be using throughout the book that I think is an extremely accurate comparison to our situation, as citizens of the U.S. In the end, if our country does well, we all stay afloat. If it sinks, we all go down with it.

―――――――――――

"No man who ever held the office of president would congratulate a friend on obtaining it."

―Former president John Adams in a letter to a relative about his son, John Quincy Adams, being elected president

―――――――――――

CHAPTER 3

What's Going On Down There?

NOW THAT WE HAVE OUR PERSPECTIVE HIGH above it all, we need to take a new look at what forces are at play every day, both in our own lives and in our government.

Everyone is working in some way or another to survive better in life. That's nothing new, right? But what I think we don't always understand is that *everything* people do, *every* decision they make and *every* action they take, is an effort to survive better. Of course, it's easy to see that the mother who feeds her child the best baby food is doing so to be a good mother and do all she can to help her child grow to be intelligent, healthy and happy. We can also easily see that a pro athlete who trains at the gym daily is working hard to survive better on the playing field, or maybe to get a lucrative contract extension for more money at the end of the season.

But what about the actions of a criminal? Does a bank robber really think stealing money is going to improve his chances of making it in the world? Absolutely, without a question. Oh, he may know that robbing the bank is risky, that it's against the law and that he might get caught. That may be very real to him, but in the end, he robs the bank because in his world, from his perspective, it's a way for him to survive better. The money he'll get will help pay his bills, cover his children's school tuition, pay for his wife's surgery or maybe get him more drugs so he can feel good one more time.

Years ago, I volunteered for a group that went into juvenile prisons in Los Angeles and worked with the worst offenders to help rehabilitate them by teaching life skills many of them were devoid of. The kids we primarily focused on were young (ages twelve to sixteen) minority males, almost all gang members and almost all going to trial for murder. Sometimes we would give a seminar, and other times we'd speak to them one-on-one. Prison guards were always present and ready to intervene if any of the inmates became aggressive.

One young man I had the pleasure of talking to was fourteen years old and grew up in East Los Angeles. He was slight in build, had a pleasant face and could have been any kid you might see in the park riding a bike or skateboarding. But this young man had killed someone. It was a fact I found incredibly hard to believe and continually had to remind myself about. Out of my immense disbelief that this gentle kid could do anything to hurt anyone, I directly asked him why he was in prison. Without emotion or hesitation, he simply told me that he had killed a guy. He wasn't trying to intimidate me, show his bravado or prove to me that he was a man. He was just simply stating a fact.

It's one thing to see a scene like that in a movie or on TV, but I can tell you that it's entirely another thing when it's real and happening in front of you. To sit across from someone—in this case, a *child*—who has actually taken someone else's life tends to stir a bit of terror in your mind. In that moment, it didn't matter how innocent, safe or friendly he looked, or that guards were watching nearby—my heart rate jumped a bit.

I asked him what had happened. He said he had gotten out of the driver's side of a car and suddenly felt something hit him and noticed that there was something hitting the car door. When he looked down the street, he saw flashes of light and somewhere in his mind realized it was a gun firing, and that it was firing at him. He said he pulled a gun out of his pocket and fired back, not knowing if he had hit anything. Next thing he knew, he was in a hospital and was told that he had killed the person who had shot him. He said the incident had lasted only a few moments. But in those few moments, his life changed forever; it wasn't possible for him to prove that the other person had shot at him first. In the end, he was in a gang, he had a gun on him and he didn't even have a driver's license for the car he had been driving.

We all hear about gangs and the shootings that take place in the bad parts of our cities. Movies and TV shows usually depict those involved as bad, evil people. And maybe they are. But the same rule of survival applies to them as it applies to the rest of us: everything they do is an effort to improve their chance of survival in life. That young man was in a gang because he wanted to live. He probably believed that he wouldn't survive long if he wasn't part of a group of other young men, especially in the neighborhood where he lived. From his perspective, carrying a gun was just smart, the same way many of us think having car insurance is smart. To shoot back at someone shooting at you—at someone trying to kill you—is certainly an act that can only be seen as survival-motivated.

I don't know about you, but when I see the plight of people living in war-torn countries, or hear of parents worried about raising their children in a gang-infested area of a city, I think, "Why don't they just move somewhere else?" Why didn't this young man just move out of South L.A. to Santa Monica, where it's safer? Or to San Diego, or one of the cities named as the safest in the country—Franklin, Massachusetts? Then he wouldn't be constantly faced with those tough life-or-death choices and find himself in prison for murder. But the world he was born in, where his friends and family lived, where he went to school, where he strove for survival every day, was no different from the world we live in, where we interact with our friends and families and strive to survive in our lives. Just as his world is foreign to you, your world is foreign to him. He goes through his life trying to survive just like you do, like we all do. This isn't to say that there isn't right versus wrong from the perspective of society, but when it comes down to the individual, *every* decision is designed in some way to improve survival.

So what does this have to do with our government? What if we took this survival motivation concept and compared it to the choices made by our elected leaders—the members of the House of Representatives, the senators, even the president? This is where it can get difficult, because most people already have a fixed view of politicians and the decisions they make. Many people think they're "crooks," that they're only there to enrich themselves, that they're trying to destroy our country, that they get into office and then they change and forget about us. Even if you don't think this about *all* elected officials, I would bet that you've had these kinds of thoughts at least once or twice about some politician at some time.

I'm not here to defend the actions of our government leaders, but I am here to ask you to consider that *everyone* and *anyone* only does those things they feel will improve their survival in some way.

Take a second to apply this idea to politicians. How do their actions, those things that many of us label as terrible and awful, help them survive better? Sure, maybe some decisions do bring them more money, but don't we all strive for that? Maybe some of the decisions help their friends, but don't we all want to help our friends? Do you think maybe some of their decisions are made to help the country? At least from *their* perspective? Could it be possible?

This is a very important step along our path to finding the reset button. I'm not asking you to think that our elected officials are all good, pure and well-intentioned. I'm only asking you to realize that each and every one of them is only acting in a way that they feel will improve their survival, either in the short or long term. I'm only asking you to see that they are human and citizens of this country, like us.

No, realizing this doesn't fix anything. But as we go forward, having this simple understanding of why they act the way they do may help give you a new perspective on how we can go about improving their decisions, which affect us all. And in the end, that's all we're really after, right? To have our country be a place where we can pursue life, liberty and happiness? Well, having an understanding of why our leaders act the way they do is important in deciding whether to push the reset button or not.

"Some of my colleagues who are criticized today for lack of forthright principles—or who are looked upon with scornful eyes as compromising 'politicians'—are simply engaged in the fine art of conciliating, balancing and interpreting the forces and factions of public opinion, an art essential to keeping our nation united and enabling our Government to function."

—President John F. Kennedy in his book *Profiles in Courage*

CHAPTER 4

Let the Games Begin

SKILL. KNOWLEDGE. CHALLENGE. COMPETITION.
Struggle. Fight. Contest. Work. Rewards. Prizes. Pay-off. Victory.

All of these are strong terms in our society, and we could come up with many more to describe much of what goes on in our lives every day.

We use whatever skills or knowledge we have to achieve what we want in life. Competition is a constant to one degree or another, whether we're competing for someone's attention, a position on a team, a slot at a school, a job or a significant other, or just acquiring enough to eat and a place that's safe to sleep. We battle against others at work, in court, in business and on the playing field. For leisure, many enjoy playing cards, competing against the odds in Vegas or being part of the weekly football pool at work.

But it doesn't stop there. Even in those moments when we're not actively engaged in some kind of competition of our own, we cheer for those engaged in theirs. Millions of people watch football, basketball, hockey, soccer or one of the myriad other sports played around the world. Huge stadiums are built at massive expense to seat thousands of spectators, who pay a great deal to watch highly skilled professionals face off in extreme competition. Back in the days of the Romans, spectators flocked to huge arenas to watch men battle each other in the ultimate competition of all, where defeat usually meant death.

And if that wasn't enough, in order to fill our lives with even more of the drama of competition, we love to read suspense novels or stories about the latest battle between man and vampire, or secret agent and evil enemy. We spend billions going to movies to see our favorite star battle a giant robot or fight off the other suitors in a quest to win the love of another character.

Why all this competition, all this battling, all this drama? Why do we engage in it ourselves, and spend our valuable time watching it and reading about others engaged in it?

For the end result, of course. We're ultimately looking for the pay-off, the prize. In every situation, we're looking for whatever we consider to be victory. Sometimes it might be money to buy food and clothing, acquire a better car or home, travel, make investments or acquire any of the other multitude of things that can be had in our world. In some situations, our goal may be to simply hold a trophy or win a ribbon or be labeled the best. In other situations, it's about the pride of being the victor, even if just for a moment, even if only against your friend in a game of tennis or the latest video game.

If we consider it for a moment, I think we'll realize that almost everything that happens in life is a kind of contest of one kind or another. It's what we're constantly engaged in. But just because we're fighting or competing in some cases for very positive things like more money, someone we love or a better home, not all contests are beneficial. War is the extreme, with one side trying to destroy the other. But war between two countries or two ideologies is fundamentally no different from the Seahawks taking on the Packers, the Lakers facing off against the Celtics or you trying to beat out the next person for that promotion at work. True, the end results aren't the same, but the goal of victory, achievement and acquiring something of value is.

So why all this in a book about fixing our government? Well, let me ask you this: What does it take to hold a contest of any kind? You need at least two sides in opposition, right? You need at least two tennis players in order to have a match. You need at least two basketball players in order to have some kind of game. There can't be a wrestling, boxing or martial arts contest without at least one person squaring off against another. Two teams are needed to play a football game.

Okay, so let's take a look at elements that are in opposition in our government. Well, to start, don't we commonly think of the situation with our government as "us" versus "them"? In fact, isn't that the entire premise of this book—that "we" need to take action against "them"? Then what about the constant battle between the Senate and the House? Or the president versus Congress? Or Congress versus the Treasury?

When you consider the battles that occur every moment of every day in our government in Washington D.C., what's the biggest contest of them all? Wouldn't it be the contest between the parties? Democrats versus Republicans, Republicans versus Democrats—every day, all the time, in every decision. I'm not here to say that one side is better than the other. Or that any of the other dozens of parties are good or bad. My goal is to show you the reset button and help you see what I see, and how we can change what's going on with our government.

The contest between parties, primarily between Republicans and Democrats, *dominates* the interactions between our elected officials. The clash of the two parties, and the quest by each to dominate the other and "win" whatever it is each side feels will be the end result, is a primary driver in what decisions are made, what laws are passed, what taxes are levied, what funds are expended and who is the beneficiary of it all.

Remember, it's vital in our quest to find the reset button that we take a giant step back from it all and get a broad, exterior perspective of what's going on, because sometimes when fully engaged in a contest or game we can actually *forget* that it's *only* a game. We can lose sight of the fact that we're simply in a contest against our best friend and not some mortal enemy during an all-out match of tennis. We can forget that our competition for that promotion at work is also a hard-working employee and not the reincarnation of the Wicked Witch of the West. And in that ultimate contest called war, we think of our enemies as bad, depraved evildoers, when in truth they are humans trying to make their way in life, just like us, with mothers, fathers, brothers, sisters and children, and who are *simply* our opponents in a contest. Sometimes we can miss the fact that in whatever endeavor or struggle we're fighting for, it's simply a contest between two or more sides for some kind of end result.

In no way am I trying to minimize the importance of the various struggles we're all engaged in. Our country wouldn't be here if it weren't for a war we waged with Great Britain in the late 1700s. It was our side and point of view against theirs, and in the end we won.

But it's interesting to note that the war was between those who wanted to break away from Great Britain, and those who didn't. We say that it was the Americans or rebels or colonists against the British. The point is, *there were two sides.* Those wanting to break away were united against those who didn't. And when the war was over, those wanting to break away had won. The two sides went their separate ways (at least for a period of time). The competition was over. Everyone was now primarily on the *same* side, and the country was trying to figure out how to form itself to survive on its own. The once-united colonies—now called states—no longer had a big formidable foe to compete against, so what did they do? They began to compete against *each other.* Some states wanted to make exclusive trade agreements with foreign countries that would cut out the other states. Many, if not all, were printing their own money and rejecting the money used by their neighbors. They went from working together as a single unit to acting in many ways like independent countries *against* each other.

And of course we know the rest of the story—a group of fifty-five people dedicated a summer in Philadelphia to writing our Constitution, which was then approved by all the states.

But it should be noted that nowhere in the Constitution is there any mention of political parties. When George Washington was elected as our first president, there were no parties. For both of the terms he served, he was elected unanimously (even though he didn't want the position) and had no opposition. It's interesting that parties started to emerge shortly after he was elected for his first term. We no longer had our attention focused on a big enemy (Great Britain). That contest was finished. But, loving competition, people naturally chose sides and began to battle each other—*through new political parties.*

And we've been battling amongst ourselves ever since. It's gotten to the point that today, when almost anything is reported regarding Congress, it's put in terms of Democrats or Republicans. Instead of letting us know that Senator John Doe thinks X or Y, it's reported that Republican or Democratic Senator John Doe thinks X or Y. This may be naive, but I've always been astounded that once the president of our country is sworn into office, he continues to be and act as a member of his political party and openly targets the opposing party. It's always been my point of view that the president should represent everyone, not just the party he belongs to, and thus should be above the fray of the battle between the parties.

President Washington was so concerned about the rise of political parties that he made special mention of them in his farewell address to the American people at the end of his presidency. He said that even though political parties "may now and then answer popular ends, they are likely in the course of time and things, to become potent engines, by which cunning, ambitious, and unprincipled men will be enabled to subvert the power of the people and to usurp for themselves the reins of government . . . " He was concerned about party spirit that tends to take over a person, and felt that it was "the interest and duty of a wise people to discourage and restrain it."[1]

Based on what we've discussed in this chapter, the emergence of parties is entirely natural and part of our constant involvement in contest, one against the other. It's how we work. But that doesn't mean we can't *understand* that parties are just that—a way of being in

---

[1] Yale Law School Lillian Goldman Law Library, "Washington's Farewell Address 1796."

contest with each other. It makes for great drama that in turn makes for wonderfully dramatic headlines. It allows us to be on a side against others. It allows us to fight against an opposition for ideas and desires we care about. Maybe all of this is good, beneficial and healthy . . . I don't know. But I do know that political parties are an extremely powerful force in our government, and if they were entirely good and helpful, then our government would be doing a fantastic job and be in great shape. Since this isn't the case, it might be wise to at least question what role our infighting plays in that.

There's one more important point that needs to be brought up while we're discussing the subject of fighting amongst ourselves: how our enemies benefit from it. Our elected officials have been designated by us to run our country. They go to D.C. and proceed to fight against each other, one side constantly trying to outdo the other. So where is our government's attention mainly focused? It's focused on itself, trying to defend and fight the opposing party.

Are we alone on this planet? Are there not over 190 other countries around the world, some (if not many) of which would love to overtake us both economically and militarily? Not to mention the various factions and groups across the globe that hate the U.S.? Don't we have strong enough adversaries outside our borders that are formidable enough to give us a big enough game to play so we don't have to square off and battle against each other? If there were, and they threatened our safety and the survival of our country, I'm sure we would quickly scrap the battle of Democrats versus Republicans, and take up the battle of the United States versus the enemy.

We saw this in play after 9/11, when people brought out their American flags and hung them like never before with incredible national unity, regardless of party. The fight between the parties seemed minor in the face of our nation being attacked. We were the United States of America, united and standing tall and strong against any and all foreign adversaries.

It's an issue that needs to be considered. Distracting your enemy can be a very effective strategy. It's used in wartime with good success. Just because we aren't officially at war with another country doesn't mean we have no enemies, and that they aren't working against us. So why do we distract ourselves with our constant internal battles that, in the end, surely must benefit those who oppose us around the world?

That's a question we'll have to leave for another time and place, since it exceeds the relevance of this book. But what is relevant, and the primary point of this chapter, is that we love to be involved in conflict, contest, games and drama. Our government is constantly engaged in this drama by way of political parties. This is vital to understand as we move forward in search of how we can improve our country's future.

"There is nothing which I dread so much as a division of the republic into two great parties, each arranged under its leader, and concerting measures in opposition to each other. This, in my humble apprehension, is to be dreaded as the greatest political evil under our constitution."

—John Adams in a letter to a friend
written on October 2, 1780

CHAPTER 5

The Test

THE NEXT VITAL STEP IN THIS JOURNEY IS clarifying exactly who you are and what role you play in our country. This will primarily apply directly to you if you're a United States citizen.

For most of my life, I've felt that I've had a very small role in what happens in our government. I've always voted in the important national elections but have occasionally skipped some of the local ones, sometimes not even knowing an election was taking place. Overall I've felt that it's been my duty and privilege to vote and do my part, though I've never felt that it made much of a difference.

But not long ago, as our government was on the verge of not increasing its debt ceiling and thus rendering itself unable to pay interest to those it had borrowed from, I had a moment of clarity. At that moment, it became incredibly clear to me that *no one* was in control of our government, and it seemed to me to be like a runaway train, heading along a set of tracks that ended at a cliff. In that instant, I realized that our elected officials weren't getting the job done and everything wasn't going to somehow work itself out. For my entire life up to that one moment, I had felt that "they" had it all under control, and that no matter how bad it seemed, our country would be fine and our American way of life would just continue indefinitely. We seemed to have worked our way through many tight spots in the past, going all the way back to World War II. Vietnam was bad, but we extracted ourselves from that and learned from it (or so I hoped). Then we had the Gulf War, Afghanistan and Iraq, and for whatever reason, I stayed fairly unconcerned, believing that our government had it all under control. This doesn't necessarily mean I agreed with all that our government did, but I still trusted that things were well in hand.

If at this point I'm on the edge of losing you because you can't believe I trusted our government for as long as I did, I understand. I don't have a good explanation other than I wanted things to be all right, so I just hoped and assumed they would be.

That all changed for me when I found that I just couldn't ignore what was happening anymore. I started searching for some kind of solution, a way to adjust things and redirect our country down a path with more longevity than the path we were, and still are, traveling.

As I looked at our government, our elected leaders, the giant lobby industry, corporations, billionaires, the media and all the other forces that seem to be at play in shaping what our government does, it all seemed so incredibly complicated and overwhelming. It seemed impossible—and possibly delusional—to find anything I could do to help create positive change in our government. Everything just seemed so immovable, powerful and unreachable.

But I personally believe that a solution can always be found for *any* seemingly immovable situation. I believe every problem, big or small, no matter how solid, can be unstuck and moved into a better condition. Some problems and situations will resolve easier than others, but I believe that they all have an Achilles heel—a vulnerability that normally remains obscured, but when found, easily brings about some degree of resolution.

With this in mind, I persisted. How could I, and others like me who were concerned about their country but had no ties to power in Washington, do *anything* to bring about a course correction for our country?

There's no need to walk you through everything I researched and read, but I will tell you that it took many, many months of work. Finally, the truth of the situation started revealing itself to me. The complexity started to fall away. The problem didn't seem so overwhelming anymore. For the first time in a long time, I started to get a little excited, because a sliver of a solution seemed to be showing itself to me.

I had bushwhacked my way through a dense jungle of noise, lies, misinformation, propaganda, opinion and misdirection that surrounded the basic truth of the entire matter. And then, there I stood, the jungle behind me and a shining piece of truth sitting quietly in front of me. But it didn't look like much. It didn't seem like much of a discovery. I was frustrated, because it was something I had already known—it didn't seem to reveal anything new to me at all. So I discarded it and continued my research.

Ultimately, I was looking for a foundational, underlying truth about our government that was *completely* unshakable—the linchpin that held all the rest of it in place.

I realized that any idea even close to being a possible solution would have to have these four traits:

1. Was it simple? I knew that if I really had the right solution, it would be easy to do. Usually the most powerful ideas are the simplest.

2. Was it something anyone could do? The solution wouldn't work if only elected officials could do it, or the president was the only one who could pull it off. My thinking on this was simple: If they hadn't done it up to this point, why would they do it now? I felt that the solution had to be something so easy and powerful, virtually anyone could do it.

3. Would it, if implemented correctly, actually, for real, cause positive change?

4. Was it something I could do something about? If it wasn't, then *who* was going to do it? It's easy to come up with ideas that someone

else should do, but the real test for me was whether *I* could execute it. If not, then it was a poor idea.

It's important to remember, when looking for an answer, that many things *can* be done that would cause activity, commotion, busywork, etc. But it's vital to assess whether or not the action would actually bring about the *end result* you're after. In every situation there may be lots of possible courses of action, but usually only one or two, if done well, will solve the real problem.

For example, here are some ideas that could be implemented in an attempt to change our country's future course:

STORM THE WHITE HOUSE: This is an idea that I think sits in the back of many people's minds because it seems simple. We're mad at the government, so let's just go take over. Disgruntled populations have done this throughout history. At the start of the French Revolution in the late 1700s, the upset population stormed and took over the Bastille, a symbolic government building and prison in Paris.

In movies and on TV, we see images of citizens of other countries who are upset with the U.S., storming our embassy in some foreign land. When people are upset, they want to take action and do something real, thus we see rioters burn buildings, tip over cars and attack innocent bystanders. When people are angry, they rarely pick the correct source of the problem to attack. Instead, their energy is directed at almost anything in front of them. Storming the White House or Capitol would be no different. Besides people dying in the process, what else would it accomplish? If we throw out our president, what then? Do we start over and rewrite the Constitution? We already did this when we got rid of King George by way of the Revolutionary War. We threw him, and the authority of Great Britain, out of the colonies and drew up our own constitution and went our own way. Since this has already been done, it seems senseless to do it again.

MOBILIZE A GIANT PROTEST: This method of causing change is used frequently with mixed results. The massive marches and public protests over civil rights and Vietnam in the 1960s forced the government to pay attention to the issue, and were helpful in changing government policy. A more recent protest called the Occupy movement was put into action by large masses of people in many cities across the country and the world. Frustrated by poor economic conditions, people simply gathered together in a common area and set up camp. The protesters wanted more economic equality, among other things. Though this movement garnered a great deal of attention, I think it's fair to say that it brought about little change. Protests can be especially effective for segments of the population that have clearly been discriminated against or deprived of some right, like in the early 1900s, when women took to the streets to protest their lack of the right to vote in elections.

As I looked at mobilizing a protest as a possible solution, I couldn't see how I was going to get enough people to give up time from their jobs, families and other activities to travel to a specific location for a march. I also couldn't see how a protest would do any good. I threw this option out very quickly.

START A PETITION ONLINE: Over the years, I've received many requests to sign this or that petition for very good causes, and many times I have. Sometimes it's helpful to show that a movement has thousands or millions of signatures behind it. But I've seen so many smart people and organizations put forth petitions, pushing for important and positive changes to our government's various policies and actions, with little actual effective results. If they couldn't make this work, how could I? I threw this idea out, too.

RUN FOR CONGRESS: At one point in my search, I seriously had to look at this approach. I couldn't see how else I could make much change in our government unless I was a part of it. If I really wanted to do something to help our country, my thinking went, I would have to just be part of the problem and fix it from the inside.

Then I started remembering all the various congressmen and senators I'd read about who had written excellent reform legislation that either never got passed or was watered down so much in the process that it essentially became ineffective. For example, of all the various congressional actions put forth to reform campaign financing or balance the budget, none of them fully solved the problem.

As I looked at this idea, many negatives surfaced:

1. Did I want to run for Congress? The answer was no.

2. If I did want to, could I actually get elected? Highly, highly doubtful, but people win the lottery so you never know.

3. Would it cause effective change? If other powerful congress persons or senators hadn't been able to truly improve aspects of our government in the past, why would it be any different for me?

4. Was this solution simple? Definitely not.

5. Could anyone do it? No way. In the end, I discarded this idea as well.

START A MOVEMENT: I almost did this, and still may at some point. My plan was to start a movement of people actively making changes in their lives, both big and small. The changes could be to their weight, relationships, job, the community they live in or even their country. I thought that if I could help enough people learn how to create change, and if they actually carried out that change and gained the confidence that comes with such victories—whether minor or massive—then our country would improve as well (or so my thinking went).

I looked over my life to figure out what steps I'd taken to successfully make change. As I said earlier in this book, years ago I wanted to push back against the out-of-control paparazzi, and so I formed the Paparazzi Reform Initiative. Through that non-profit, I've been able to reach millions about the importance of personal privacy, and I've directly helped get four privacy laws passed in the California Legislature. I've also worked with some of the most successful people in their fields.

Looking over what I had done and what I'd seen others do to make positive change, I came up with a series of steps that, when put into action, had led to a desired change. The steps were applicable to any kind of change someone wanted to make in their life, whether it was their health, relationships, job or anything else. I registered the website TimeToDisagree.com, and even had a video done of me going over each point.

Even though I liked this approach, because I enjoy helping people in general, I just didn't see how it was going to cause real change in our country fast enough. So I left it on the shelf to possibly take up at another time.

In the end, I discarded all of these ideas and, frustrated, wondered if there really was anything that I could do—or that anyone could do—to bring about enough change in our government to actually put the country back on a healthy, lasting path. I felt defeated and powerless. If all the various things people all over the U.S. did every day to improve our government couldn't markedly change the direction of our country, how could I ever hope to do so?

Like a tiny ember glowing in the midst of a fire long dead, that basic truth I spoke of earlier—the one I had considered too simple to have any real value or power—festered quietly in my mind. Eventually, I gave it another look. I held it up and looked at it in the light. I prodded it to see how it would respond. I evaluated it against the four traits I had determined were necessary for a real solution. I put it through a number of hypothetical scenarios to see if it held up.

The result of all this? I was astounded to find that this little simple truth held up to every test I put it through, withstood every scenario I could think up and fulfilled all the traits of a bona fide solution. Over days, then weeks and then months, I kept mentally putting the idea through various scenarios to test—at least in theory—its workability. And over time, as it passed all of my tests again and again, I grew excited.

This seemingly "too simple" truth is at the cornerstone of our Constitution. It is what gives the document its power—the reset button installed in it by those who wrote it. If properly used, it has the legal power to simply allow us—the citizens—to peacefully and quickly overthrow our government whenever we feel such action needs to be taken to ensure its health and longevity.

This truth is something that, if carried out properly, we can use to alter our country's course toward a better future. But as I uncover it for you, remember how difficult it was for me to believe in its power and value. You may discount it at first, too. However, if you test it as I did, you'll see its power as I do and together we can take action to improve our country's future.

"Truth will ultimately prevail where there is pains taken to bring it to light."

—President George Washington in a letter written on August 10, 1794, to his neighbor, who had also served under him as an officer during the Revolutionary War

---

CHAPTER 6

The unshakable Truth

WHEN WE WANT TO GET DOWN TO THE BOTTOM of any problem, anything that doesn't seem to be going right or looks unfixable, we need to look for and find *truth*.

It isn't always easy to see at first, usually because we're either not looking for it, or we're looking in the wrong place. But in the end, everything is built on some kind of foundational truth. And once that truth is spotted, solutions become apparent, problems cease to exist and things tend to improve.

As I mentioned in the last chapter, I stumbled across a piece of truth, but it didn't look like much and didn't seem to help fix the problem, so I left it behind. Instead, I started moving forward with TimeToDisagree.com.

But that nugget of truth kept nagging at me, and eventually I couldn't ignore it. When I looked at it again, I realized what I had found wasn't just any truth—it was *the* unshakable basic truth about our country that I'd been searching for. I had overlooked it because I couldn't see exactly how to harness it and actually use it to bring about change. But after looking at many other approaches and ideas to fix our government, I recognized it for what it was—the *only* force capable of changing anything in our government.

This truth was put in place as the *foundation* of our Constitution by those who wrote it. It's what gives our government *power*. No, it isn't the Supreme Court. This power is greater than even that. It isn't the president or Congress. This power far oversteps theirs. And it doesn't reside with our military. It's even bigger than that.

The ultimate power in our country? It is *you*.

It may not always seem like it, but if you're a citizen of our country, you are more powerful than the president, Congress and the Supreme Court combined. You're even more powerful than our Constitution, because only you can change it. Yes—you!

I know this sounds all too simple, but hear me out. Let's take a closer look at this, because we can't ignore this one fact: it's *truth*. Others may have you think that you're really not that powerful or you don't matter, but truth can't be ignored. It can be covered up, buried or obscured, but it can't be extinguished. The truth is this: our Constitution, the very document that gives our government its right to exist, clearly and unequivocally states that *you* oversee it, not the other way around.

The truth is that you are one of the most powerful people on earth today. You have the power to elect someone to represent you in the most powerful government on the planet. You get to decide who speaks for you in that government. No one else in the world has that power.

Whether you're rich like Bill Gates, or the poorest person living on the streets, you get a say in who runs this country. In fact, everyone's vote is equal; your vote carries just as much weight as Mr. Gates's vote.

Look, there are seven billion people on earth. Everything the U.S. government does—what it spends, what it does militarily, how it treats the environment—in some way, at some point, will most likely affect every one of them. In the U.S., approximately 225 million people are eligible to vote. That means seven billion people across the world who are affected by the U.S. leaders' decisions have no say in who those leaders are.

But you do. You have a power that others *wish* they had. You are *powerful*.

Why are millions of dollars spent on political advertising by candidates, corporations, billionaires and others? And *who* are those advertisements directed toward? You! Every penny, all the work done to craft those messages, all the research—all of it is done to influence *you*.

Over six *billion* dollars was spent on the 2012 congressional and presidential campaigns.[1] And every penny of it was spent in some way to influence *you*. Why? Because only *you* can change our government. Only *you* can say who goes to Washington. If you are an eligible voter in our country, only *you* have the power to vote.

I know this sounds too easy, but really step back and take a look at it. We're not in the Middle Ages anymore, where some king can just do as he wishes and you don't have any power in the matter. The truth is that you have *all* the power. Corporations can't vote. Foreign governments don't get a vote. The president can't decide who will succeed him. Congress doesn't get to select who comes into office when they leave. *Only you can.*

I know what you may be thinking—you've voted before and it didn't change anything. But that only happened because you didn't vote in a way that carried enough power to bring about the change you wanted. It wasn't until I realized *how* we should use our power that I knew I'd found the true reset button.

How to press the reset button will come a little later in this book. The important point at this stage is for you to understand for yourself your true power and role in our government. We're dealing with truth here, built right into our Constitution. It isn't something we have to work toward or fight for—that was already done in the 1700s. This isn't a hope or wish or some far-off dream. This is real, it's already in place and it has massive power if used correctly.

---

[1] Federal Election Commission, "FEC Summarizes Campaign Activity of the 2011-2012 Election Cycle."

The correct way to describe your role over our government is to compare it to the role a person plays on the board of directors of a major company. Every company has a board of directors, and it's their job to ensure that the company fulfills its mission or purpose, which is usually laid down by the organization's founders. The board monitors the company's performance and makes changes in management as necessary, always keeping in mind the health of the company and its successful progress toward achieving its mission.

But it's important to understand that the board doesn't run the company, nor do the board members have to know how to run it. They only need to understand the purpose of the company and ensure that the right managers are in place to fulfill that purpose, usually at a profit. Even non-profits have to bring in more money than they spend, just like you or me, or they'll be out of business.

Ultimately, this book is about the power you wield and a new way you might use it to create the country you want.

But that's up to you, because you are the *only* one with the power to elect the leaders who then run our government. No matter what political ads air incessantly on the television or radio, or the argument your friend may have for this or that candidate, or even the bold idea outlined in this book, *no one* but *you* has the ultimate power to say who gets elected and who doesn't.

It's a good position to be in. You should congratulate yourself for being one of the few in the world who's in it.

―――――――――

"I consider the people who constitute
a society or nation as the source of all
authority in that nation."

—Secretary of State Thomas Jefferson in a formal
opinion written on April 28, 1793, regarding the
validity of treaties the U.S. had with France at the time

―――――――――

CHAPTER 7

Truth & Lies

OKAY, WE'VE FOUND A PIECE OF TRUTH THAT HAS incredible power. When those who wrote our Constitution formulated our country in a way that allowed the people to run it, they knew it was a risk. They clearly understood the power it placed in the hands of the citizens of the United States. And further, they knew others would try to influence them (and possibly even lie and deceive them) to use their power in ways that wouldn't be beneficial to the long-term health of their country.

Earlier we talked about our constant need for contest, competition and drama. Well, what better way to throw off your enemy or competition than with some good old-fashioned lies and deception? The further information gets from the truth, the closer it comes to being a lie.

It's vital to know that a piece of information can be both somewhat true and somewhat false. The tabloid press uses this to their great advantage. Having worked in the entertainment industry for as long as I have, I've seen up close and personal how they twist the truth. The latest story about that famous actress who's getting divorced from her famous husband usually doesn't turn out to be true, does it? The article may have details about someone seeing them arguing, or that the husband was living in a hotel or some other *true* piece of information. But those pieces of truth don't necessarily mean that the assumption is true—that they're getting divorced. A little bit of truth mixed in with a bunch of lies doesn't make something true.

Deception, lies, propaganda, misinformation, altered facts—these are on the other side of the spectrum from where truth lives. These are what we must constantly be on the lookout for. You have the only power over our government that exists (short of another country taking it over through military action). But you haven't always felt that way, have you? Those times that you felt powerless, or were convinced that the government had power over you, is when untruth entered the picture.

AVOID   **FIND**

◄───►

deception   truth
lies
propoganda
misinformation
altered facts

I'm not trying to paint a picture that the evil forces of the world are filling the newspapers and airwaves and Internet with lies. What I am saying is that you have *power* that others want to *control*. You're the *only* one who can legally walk into a voting center on Election Day and decide who runs our government! That moment when you mark the ballot is when the magic happens! Ballots are the *only* things that count in deciding who the managers are for our country. Not advertisements or how much money was spent. Not some king or military tribunal. The *only* thing that counts is that ballot containing your selection.

Every ad that you get in the mail, or that you see on TV or the Internet, is designed to influence you when you enter the voter's booth. Those messages are solely designed to guide your fingers to mark the box that *they* think is best. They want to be in that booth *with* you when you make your decision. They want their message playing in your mind to influence how you vote.

So, with all that's at stake—after all, you aren't picking the managers of a local street beautification organization, you're picking the managers of the most wealthy and powerful government in the world—do you think you might be told a few lies, half truths, and deceptions? Remember, what we're after here is the truth, not what we wish was the truth. Not every political ad is untrue, but some most definitely are. Some have a little truth and a lot of deception, and some have lots of truth and a little deception. And some are actually true.

But unless you realize the power you have, you may not realize that others will do *anything* to get you to see things their way. The color of an ad, the attractiveness of the candidates in them and the apparent soundness of their arguments don't necessarily add up to a message that is true. It's vital to understand whether the entire message, in the context it's being delivered, is true or not. That ad may sound alarming, inspirational or truthful. The voice in it may sound just like a nice grandfather. The editorial in the paper may appear very neutral and thorough. But all of that must be filtered out, so the only thing being considered is this: Is the message mostly true or mostly false? It takes practice to filter out all of the unimportant extra parts of a message, but it's vital to separate the truth from the not-so-true.

One very real experience I had with this relates back to that same senator I interned for in college. When I left that summer, I had another year and a half of college to get through before I could graduate. Before I left DC, the senator told me that he'd have a job for me on his staff if I wanted it when I graduated. So I returned to school with that intention in mind. But the senator had to win an election the November before I completed my studies, which was in December. The timing couldn't have been better—I would start my new position with him at the beginning of his new six-year term in office.

The challenger for his Senate seat was very organized and well-funded. It was a heated campaign and a very close race. In the last week before the election, the senator's opponent ran a TV ad on all the stations in the state. The ad implied that the senator had voted against senior citizens—a very important block of voters that had traditionally backed him. The problem was that the ad carried some truth and a good deal of untruth, and the overall effect was devastating. In the end, the senator lost the election by a very narrow margin. And I was out of a job before I'd even started.

There are two general kinds of false information to be aware of: 1) false information given out by mistake and 2) false information given out on purpose.

1.   The first category is information we receive from some source that's wrong. They didn't intend for it to be wrong—maybe they thought it was correct—but in the end it just wasn't true. This could be as simple as the nightly news accidentally reporting someone's name wrong, or the weatherperson promising sunshine today when instead it rains. This also includes someone saying they know how to fix your car but in the end, they break it further. In general, the person or organization putting out this category of information doesn't mean to deceive anyone—they just get it wrong.

2.   The second category is just the opposite of the first. Here you have people and/or organizations putting out information that is untrue on purpose. They're lying. They're intentionally trying to cause some kind of an effect—whether it's to make something happen or to stop something from happening. The examples that fall under this category are endless. A company reports that they have $100 million in income, when in fact they've lost $100 million. A person steals some money from you, but when confronted, they say they didn't. One country might publicly announce that they have no plans to

invade another country, when in fact they're invading at that very moment. This is the category we need to look a little deeper into, to find what's behind the intentionally false information. When a crime occurs, police are trained to look for the motive. They look for some reason someone might have to commit that crime. It's pretty rare for any crime to be committed without a motive. Likewise, it's rare for someone to lie without a reason.

The biggest trick is *knowing* when the person isn't being entirely truthful. We've all been deceived by someone who says such and such is true, when in fact it isn't, and they know it.

But what can be extra difficult is that sometimes the person doing the lying has convinced themselves so well why that lie is okay that they believe what they're saying is true or, at the minimum, they've convinced themselves that telling that lie is okay. They have it completely justified in their mind. And one of the saddest aspects of this is that once a person has started down that path of telling some information that isn't true, it's incredibly difficult to reverse course and come clean. One small lie leads to another, which leads to another, until the person must now do everything they can to make it look like the lie is actually true. Because if they don't, they'll be found wrong—something none of us ever wants. In the end, we all want to be right.

So, when assessing information, it's important to:

1. Inspect it first and decide for yourself whether it's true for you or not.

2. Consider your own experience with similar information and whether it worked for you in the past when you used it.

3. Think about what source the information is coming from and whether that person or organization has a history of giving out good

or bad information, and if it makes *sense* that they are the source of the information based on their job, background or education.

4. Take a look at whether the person might be innocently misinforming you, or if they're twisting the information in some way for a particular purpose that isn't disclosed, even if it looks like they're completely convinced it's true.

I can't emphasize the importance of this enough, not only on our journey to finding the reset button, but also in our everyday lives.

We're ultimately in charge of our country, and if things aren't going right, we must separate the lies from the truth so we can take the best course of action to put things back on track.

———————————

"I have faith in the people. . . . The danger is, that they are misled. Let them know the truth and the country is safe."

—President Abraham Lincoln during an interview with a reporter in July 1864

———————————

CHAPTER 8

we, the Group called Americans

As WE'VE DISCUSSED, IF YOU'RE AN AMERICAN citizen with the right to vote, you're automatically on the board of directors of our country. It's not something you need to sign up for or join, and you don't have to have a certain IQ, have gone to a top university, belong to the right club or be of a certain sex, color or belief system to be on the board. Just by being a U.S. citizen and qualifying to vote, you're on the board *automatically*. And, as a member, you're part of a very select and important group. But the thing to note here is that you're *part* of that group, whether you choose to participate in it or not. The only way to leave the group is if you renounce your citizenship or do something that makes you ineligible to vote.

This is a hugely important point that we need to take a closer look at, because ultimately it means the difference between us running our country and someone else or some other group running it. Let me assure you that there are *plenty* of people and organizations that would *gladly* step in to be the overseers of our government, if we aren't going to do the job ourselves.

Let's take a look at this at a basic level. We have some seven billion people living on earth right now, spread out in various densities across the landmasses on the planet. Those people are currently living in one of about 195 countries. Each country has some form of government. As we learned earlier, the word "government" comes from a Greek word that means "to steer." The government's job is to steer things for the citizens of that country. This has most commonly been done throughout history by a single individual—a king, queen, czar, pharaoh or someone else carrying a similar title. But in the late 1700s, something very strange and unusual happened—we broke away from Great Britain and set up a government not run by one person, but by the *people*.

Listen, I know this is old news and something everyone knows, but it's important that we get the right perspective on this. Setting up a government in a way that allowed the *people* to rule was very unusual and unproven at that time. It was a system of governing that had only worked a couple of times before in history, and even then it didn't endure. As I said before, the usual way of governing throughout history has been for an *individual* to rule *over* the people. That seems to be the more natural inclination of running a group. In business, the owner rules and says how the company will be managed. And whether we agree with it or not, throughout history families have traditionally been run by the oldest male.

It's much easier to have one individual running things, because it takes a lot more effort and time to run an organization in a way where everyone has an equal vote. Additionally, the individual members of the group may not have the unique vision, perspective and strength of the leader.

Ever since we put in place a government overseen by the people—not just one person—many countries around the world have adopted similar forms of government. According to the Economist Group, over half the countries in the world allow their citizens, to a greater or lesser degree, a say in their government.[1] But over fifty countries *still* don't give their citizens any voice.

As I explained earlier, it's important that we take a step back and look at things in order to get a broader, more exterior perspective of what's really going on. We occasionally need to get out of the trees and get a view of the forest as a whole.

And here's that view: For millennia, mankind has been fighting, writing and dreaming about greater freedom to control one's own destiny, to throw off the yoke of oppression by dictators and abusive monarchs. Yet well over half of us on the board that now *have* the freedom to freely say how our government should be run . . . *don't*! In 2014, during the election that included voting for all of the House of Representatives and a third of the Senate, it's estimated that 140 *million* board members didn't use their power—they didn't take advantage of this rare and unusual freedom they possess.[2] That's sixty-four percent of all board members. Out of that group, millions of men didn't vote, yet 25,000 people (mostly men) died fighting for this right in the Revolutionary War.[3] Millions of women didn't vote, yet it was a right that took over a hundred years for them to win and was granted just in the last century. Millions of black men didn't vote, a right they were

---

[1] Economist Intelligence Unit, "Democracy Index 2014."

[2] United States Election Project, "2014 November General Election Turnout Rates."

[3] Burrows, "Patriots or Terrorists?" Note: It's estimated that between 4,000 and 6,000 Americans were killed in battle during the Revolutionary War, with another 18,000 or so who died as prisoners, and still more who died as a result of disease that rapidly spread amongst the troops.

granted in 1869 after a very bloody and costly Civil War.

Imagine how much change we could make in our government if *just* those 140 million voted using the method described later in this book! We're not talking about just a few thousand or even a million— we're talking about *140 million* people who didn't participate in the last election and could have. I don't know if that hits you like it does me, but I find it incredible!

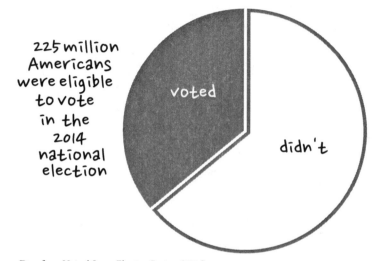

225 million Americans were eligible to vote in the 2014 national election

voted

didn't

Source: Data from United States Election Project (2014)

Why would so many not participate? There's certainly some percentage of these board members who possibly were not physically able to get to the voting booth for a variety of reasons. Then surely there were those who unexpectedly found themselves traveling or involved in urgent activities that prevented them from physically getting to the place where they could cast their ballot. And, certainly, some probably got lost, didn't know where to go or had no idea an election was even taking place.

But I believe that a vast majority of those who didn't participate, and who regularly don't vote, simply have opted out of the system. For a whole array of reasons, they've decided not to play the game. Most will say that they simply don't have time to vote, but I think the real reasons run deeper. Many may feel that their vote doesn't matter and that, no matter how they vote, the government just gets worse anyway, so why bother? Some may feel that they don't understand the issues in the election, or know anything about the various candidates running for office. This can be especially true in heavily populated areas, or if a person is new to an area and has no connection whatsoever with those on the ballot. To a large degree, we're a transient society today, and our connections with our local community have become less and less, which can result in less personal interest in local and regional elections.

In general, many may just choose *not* to participate as a subtle—or not so subtle—form of protest against the government or the "system." If a person doesn't agree with something, he or she might opt out, not participate and not acknowledge it. The truth is, non-participation can be an effective way of causing change. If enough people don't do something, then that thing or activity might fail. It's easy to see how this might work in a playground basketball game. The rules aren't being followed, the other team is making fouls for no reason, and it continues even after you and others voice your disagreement. Not only is the game no fun, it's also getting dangerous, so you decide to walk away and not play. You don't want to be party to that game anymore—you don't agree with it. And others may join you, and eventually that game will not have enough participants to continue. If that happens, the game's over.

Another good example of using non-participation as a form of protest was the case of Rosa Parks, a black woman who made history by refusing to move from her seat on the city bus in Montgomery, Alabama, in 1955. At the time, there was a law in place that black bus riders had to sit in the seats behind the first ten rows of the bus, which were reserved for white people. The law further stated that if the reserved section for white bus riders filled up, then the black bus riders would have to give up their seats and sit farther back in the bus.

Well, when Rosa got on the bus she sat behind the white section, per the law. But when it eventually filled up and she was asked to give up her seat and move farther back, she refused. She wouldn't move. She decided to no longer participate with that law. She was arrested and convicted, and when she appealed (again refusing to participate), she helped push the issue of segregation in America to the forefront. A very effective use of non-participation—it got attention and helped bring about beneficial change for black citizens across our country.[4]

Throughout the 1960s in the United States, people took to the streets and protested the Vietnam War. They were no longer going to participate in the status quo. They were no longer going to participate with how things were. It was very effective.

But there's a fundamental problem with this approach when it comes to opting out of participating in our duty as board members to oversee our government. It plays right into the hands of those who want to control the country for their own benefit. For example, if I want to influence the voters to vote a certain way, would I want many people to vote, or only a few? It makes sense that the fewer people who vote, the greater potential I have to influence them. If I only had a million dollars to convince people to vote a certain way, I could spend more per person if 100,000 people were going to vote, versus if 500,000 were going to vote, right? To take this further, if I could get all the people who were going to vote against me to *not vote at all*, then I'm more likely to win.

And how might I ensure that fewer people vote? Well, how about like this:

1. Make the issues in the election so complicated that most people can't understand them, or what the candidates think about them.

---

[4] National Archives, "Teaching with Documents: An Act of Courage, the Arrest Records of Rosa Parks."

2. Make all candidates sound, act and look the same so that in the end, it really doesn't matter who's elected.

3. Bombard potential voters with TV ads, mailers and other messages regarding the election so that they become nauseated even at the *thought* of voting.

4. Allow advertising to be less than fully truthful to cast doubt in the minds of the voters as to the integrity of the entire election system.

5. Pile on negative ads that rip other candidates down on a personal level, to give the election process a very negative flavor (and make anyone thinking of running for office reconsider whether they want to).

6. Make voting inconvenient by only holding it on a single day and not looking for ways to ensure that the maximum number of eligible voters can and do vote.

7. Release poll numbers ahead of an election that indicate a wide margin of victory for a candidate, thus making it seem as if the election has already been decided before any votes have been cast at all.

So am I actually saying that someone, or some group, is trying to dissuade people from voting? Yes and no. There are those who do everything they can to control elections, and I don't necessarily mean the politicians themselves. There are many people involved in lots of organizations working behind the scenes to control who wins and who loses. I'm not a conspiracist; I just think it's reality.

Let me put it this way: If you had the power to possibly influence an election in a way that was legal, would you? I'm sure you would.

Now, what if you had the power to influence an election in a way that was illegal? I'm betting more people would answer "yes" than they'd like to admit. And by all this, I'm not saying that some secret government agency rigs the system (that I know of). I'm just saying that individuals and organizations, some publicly known and some not, do all they can to tip the election results in their favor.

They can only do that if we allow them to, because *we're* in charge in this country. But we can only be in charge if we fulfill our duty as board members, which is to pick the managers to oversee *our* government. So opting out and not participating is *not* the solution to not agreeing with our government. Not in this case.

What is the solution? Taking fifteen minutes out of your life every couple of years, and putting into practice the ideas laid out in this book. *Participating with a smart plan in mind.*

I know that I risk testing your patience by continually pressing the point that the country is *ours* and that *we the people* are in charge. Of course *everyone* knows that! Well, I continue to bring it up because I'm not sure everyone really does know that. I think that if they really understood it, we wouldn't have more than half the board members sitting out on Election Day.

Sometimes I wonder if people who don't vote might just be stuck in a long-term cultural habit of not getting involved in governmental-type activities for fear of repercussions.

So it made me wonder: Have we as a people failed to realize that we're living in a *very* safe time compared to our past? I know this may sound silly, but could it be possible that, on some long-term cultural level, we haven't completely forgotten about the persecution that befell people who tried to make change in the past?

Just one example from history is the Inquisition, that effort by religious authorities to punish those who didn't believe as they did. If you didn't answer their questions correctly, you could be *executed*. This continued off and on from the 1100s to the 1800s—a period of *700 years*. The last person to be executed by the Inquisition was a schoolteacher in Spain because he was teaching his students about a different religion than the one approved by the government. The authorities arrested him, held him in prison for two years and then hanged him in 1826—not very long ago.[5] (No wonder the early citizens of our country demanded that "freedom of religion" be part of our Constitution!)

There are many examples in history of people being persecuted for being different, thinking differently and speaking out against the status quo. But that is the *past*. That *isn't* today. We need to realize that we live in a time of *incredible* freedoms. We can choose who we marry, where we live, what religion we are (or aren't) a part of and what we think—all without the secret police showing up to haul us away.

And most importantly, regarding which manager you choose to run our country—no one will know how you vote. It's *completely* secret. The government doesn't keep records of who you vote for. No one tracks you down years later to blame you for voting one way or the other. It's *anonymous*. It's not tracked. It's private. Hard to believe, right? But true. So really, what do you have to lose?

And on the reverse, if millions decided to vote as laid out in this book, what do you (and all of us) have to gain? *Nothing less than a new government, and one that understands that we're in charge.*

The bottom line—the actual truth of the situation—is that we oversee our government, not the other way around. That is the *foundation* of our Constitution, not some afterthought. As the overseers, if *we* don't do the overseeing, someone else certainly will. If it isn't us, then what we want for our country may not happen. If others are doing the overseeing, you can be certain that they will direct things that benefit them the most, which may not connect with

---

[5] MacNevin, "The Spanish Inquisition: Killing Non-Christians for the Mother Church."

what we think is best. Again, this isn't a situation where you need to go sign up or join a club—you're already part of the board if you're a citizen and are eligible to vote. Yes, you need to register to vote so they know you exist and where you live, but that's it. And if you still have any concern about your privacy or safety for speaking up, look around and realize that you're in the present, in a safe place and time, and not in the past.

Look, no one can force you to do your job as a board member, which is also a wonderful freedom of our country. But I urge you to consider the simple system that I'll lay out later in the book. If it's to your liking, please do participate and help us take back control of our country for the betterment of all.

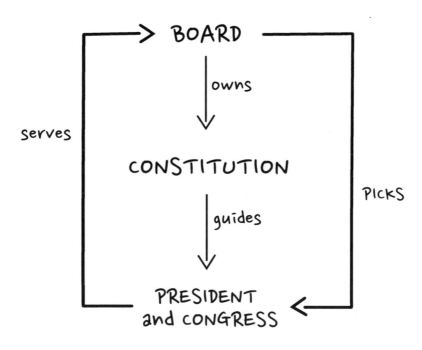

———————

"We are placing our reliance on the principle of self-government. We expect there will be mistakes, but they will be mistakes which the people themselves make, because they control their own Government. But if the people fail to vote, a government will be developed which is not their government. . . . The whole system of American Government rests on the ballot box. Unless citizens perform their duties there, such a system of government is doomed to failure."

—President Calvin Coolidge in a speech given to the Daughters of the American Revolution on April 19, 1926

———————

CHAPTER 9

The Duties of a Board

OKAY, SO YOU'RE ON THE BOARD OF DIRECTORS of the U.S. But what exactly does a board do? Let's take a short look at this.

The board of directors is simply a group of individuals with the authority to oversee the affairs of an organization. They usually don't get involved in the day-to-day activities; that's the job of the executives and managers, whom we'll simply refer to collectively as "management."

It's the duty of the board to ensure that the organization remains healthy, well-managed and moving toward its objective. The board of a company that makes tires would ensure that the company is profitable, developing improved products to introduce in the future, competing well against its competitors and complying with applicable laws and regulations. If any of these areas are suffering, the board might take action by directing the company to take on a new marketing firm, firing the chief executive officer (CEO) of the company or any number of broad actions. A board must take action, when needed, or it can be seen as negligent for not doing its job.

For a moment, assume that you're on the board of directors of an auto repair shop and the board gets together for a meeting every few months. At one of the meetings it's reported that the company is spending more than it's bringing in, which of course means it's running at a deficit, or loss. So you and the other board members inform the

CEO that he needs to get the company making money again, which he agrees to do. At the next meeting three months later, you again learn that the company is still losing money and in fact the situation has gotten much worse, not better. So again, the board meets with the CEO and hears all the reasons why the company is losing money and again demands that the CEO turn things around. Based on the current problems, the board now agrees to meet every month, to monitor the situation more closely.

At the next meeting, the company is still losing money. And at the next, and the next. At each meeting, the CEO explains why there's a loss and promises to get the shop back to making money. So at some point, what do you do? Well, one solution is to fire the CEO and hire a new one. And if that one doesn't get things fixed, you can fire that one and get another. And so on. In fact, you can do that over and over until you find someone who *will* get things turned around and get the company making money again.

Why is it so important for the company to make money? Well, it's common sense that if you don't bring in more than you spend, you need to dip into your savings to cover expenses. When the savings run dry, you have three choices: shut the shop down, borrow money to stay open or simply make more money than you're spending.

Let's assume things are still bad and you don't want to close the shop, so you borrow money to pay workers and cover other expenses. That's all fine, for a while. But now you have that extra expense of making a monthly payment on that debt. Plus you'll have to pay a bit extra in interest.

So let me ask you this: What happens if you just continue borrowing? You borrow to cover the expenses needed to keep the business open, and then you borrow to also cover the payment on the money you're borrowing. So let's say this continues. You keep borrowing, and your debt continues to grow. And your debt payment each month continues to rise, and you continue to borrow.

I think you can see the fundamental problem with this. Now I ask you, should the board of directors of the company just continue to let the borrowing continue? Is that the wise decision here? Or should the board have fired the CEO *long* ago and gotten someone in that position who *could* get the operation working again at a profit? I think the answer is pretty obvious: replace the CEO and get someone very skilled in place to turn things around.

Even if you've never been on the board of a company, or owned a company, you know—we *all* know—that you have to bring in more money than you spend or you pile on debt, and that leads to problems. Most know this from personal experience.

Even non-profit organizations have to follow this same fundamental law of nature. One very large non-profit that failed to follow this very simple rule was the Allegheny Health, Education and Research Foundation, based in Pittsburgh. With total assets over $2 billion, it failed to bring in more money than it was spending and went bankrupt in 1998.[1] This also meant the end of the largest private medical school in the country, which the foundation owned—all non-profit. Whether an organization is big or small, or whether someone is wealthy like Warren Buffet or just a family living very simply on little income, the rules apply exactly the same way: money coming in must be greater than money going out. Like the law of gravity, it works every time . . . eventually.

So those are the simple basics about boards of directors. That is their basic purpose and function. They have power that must be used to help the organization they oversee fulfill its overall purpose and stay operational.

The good news is that the individual board members don't necessarily have to have the skills themselves to run the company. They don't have to know how to make computer chips if they sit on the board of a

---

[1] Burns, "The Fall of the House of AHERF: The Allegheny Bankruptcy."

computer company, or how to make tires if they oversee a tire company. They don't even need to know how to adjust the operation to make it profitable. They simply need to understand the goals and purposes of the organization and the rule about bringing in more money than what goes out, and have some way of discerning whether the organization is healthy or not. If the board members are able to get accurate information, then their job is simply to ensure that management keeps the company making more than it spends and moving toward its goals and purposes. That's it. They don't have to figure it all out and solve all the problems. That's management's job. And if management isn't doing its job, it gets replaced with a management team that *can* get the job done.

"This country, with its institutions, belongs to the people who inhabit it. Whenever they shall grow weary of the existing Government, they can exercise their constitutional right of amending it or their revolutionary right to dismember or overthrow it."

—President Abraham Lincoln in his first inaugural address shortly after being sworn in as president on March 4, 1861

CHAPTER 10

Purpose

A GOVERNMENT, LARGE OR SMALL, IS SIMPLY AN organization. It's nothing more than a group of individuals working toward a common goal and, in the case of our national government, delivering certain services to *us*, the citizens of the country. Really, that's the simplicity of it. Someone has to build the roads, defend the country, and run the court system.

In a small village, the government might consist of a single person. Of course, as the community grows, so will the government. Our national government now consists of over four million workers. But in the end, it's just an organization with a purpose to fulfill. It also has an obligation to make sure it brings in more than it pays out so it can stay healthy and endure. More on this second point soon.

So the government is there to provide us with services and we have the ultimate authority over it, but who actually runs it? The president and Congress (both the House of Representatives and the Senate) are in charge on our behalf. Our Constitution gives us the power to choose them, and it gives them the power to oversee all aspects of our government operations. Just in case this isn't crystal clear, *they* work for *us*.

Okay, so our government, even though it's huge, is just an organization. And like any organization, it has a *purpose*. Though we might sometimes think that its purpose is to tax us incessantly or spend our money foolishly, these aren't its purposes. The purpose for our government is listed at the very beginning of our Constitution:

"We the People of the United States, in Order to form a more perfect Union, establish Justice, insure domestic Tranquility, provide for the common defence, promote the general Welfare, and secure the Blessings of Liberty to ourselves and our Posterity, do ordain and establish this Constitution for the United States of America."[1]

In order to pull out the various purposes for our government as laid out in this paragraph, let's break it down further:

1. *We the people, in order to*: The first six words of our Constitution clearly let it be known *who* is authoring the document, and that it's being authored for a particular purpose or purposes, which follow in the rest of the paragraph.

2. *form a more perfect union*: This first statement reflects the situation the original thirteen states of our country faced after declaring their independence from Great Britain on July 4, 1776. They no longer considered themselves colonies of Great Britain, but the United States of America. In reality, with Great Britain no longer their ruler, each state became, in essence, an independent nation at war. But all the former colonies, now independent, felt it wise to work together to fight off the mighty British military, the most powerful in the world at that time.

The agreement they put together and ratified was our country's first constitution, called the Articles of Confederation and Perpetual Union.[2] The problem with this document was that it was weak, but it was better than what they'd had before, which was being ruled by Great Britain. The government of the new United States of America had no single figurehead to oversee it, like our president today, nor

---

[1] In 1787 (when the Constitution was written), it was common practice to capitalize important nouns in the middle of sentences. Also at that time, "ensure" was spelled as "insure"; by the same token, the spelling of "defence" with a "c" is how the word "defense" is commonly spelled in Great Britain, both then and now.

[2] Library of Congress, "The Articles of Confederation."

did it have the power to collect taxes or the authority to print money. It did bind the states together during the war, but once it was won, a great deal of turmoil ensued, both economic and social. The country fell into a depression, and the new country had massive debt it had taken on to fight the British. Many states were printing their own money, much of which was worthless.

So the United States Congress authorized a meeting of representatives from all the states to gather in Philadelphia at the start of the 1787 summer season to fix the Articles of Confederation.[3] But when those representatives got together, instead of fixing the articles, they wrote an entirely new Constitution. Their intention for the new Constitution was to create a better way for the independent states to perpetually work together for the good of the people—to "form a more perfect union."

3. *establish Justice*: This part is fairly self-explanatory. It simply means that the government is to provide real justice for the citizens of the country.

4. *insure domestic Tranquility*: The word "domestic" of course means something occurring within the country. And "Tranquility" simply means "a state of calm." So here, the Constitution is instructing our government to make sure we don't experience chaos and uprisings within the boundaries of our own country (which had been happening in the new United States after the war with Great Britain ended).[4] The directive here is that the government is to keep order and calm within the country so we can all go about living our lives in peace.

---

[3] National Endowment for the Humanities, "Lesson 1: The Road to the Constitutional Convention."

[4] Shay's Rebellion was one uprising that occurred in the United States prior to the Constitutional Convention of 1787.

5. *provide for the common defence*: The meaning here is simply that the new national government would provide for the defense of all the states from foreign invasion (much more efficient than each state having its own army).

6. *promote the general Welfare*: Like the other points listed above, this is a very important purpose of our government and one we should make sure we fully understand, so let's look at a couple of the words in it. The word "promote" here means "to help (something) happen, develop or increase."[5] The word "welfare" means "the state of doing well especially in respect to good fortune, happiness, well-being or prosperity."[6] So, according to our Constitution, it's a core purpose of our government to help develop and increase our happiness, well-being and prosperity. Not a small task, but one assigned to our government by those who wrote the Constitution.

7. *and secure the Blessings of Liberty to ourselves and our Posterity*: "Liberty" means "the power of choosing, thinking and acting for oneself; freedom from control or restriction" and "posterity" means "future generations."[7] Simply put, another purpose of our government is to make sure the citizens of the country have the freedom to think and act as they wish, and that they're able to live without undue restriction from authority or the government, now and for future generations.

8. *do ordain and establish this Constitution for the United States of America*: "Ordain" means "to officially order."[8] So this phrase means that the *people* officially put forth and establish the document as the Constitution for our country.

---

[5] Merriam-Webster Dictionary.

[6] Ibid.

[7] Collins English Dictionary.

[8] Merriam-Webster Dictionary.

Purpose is a very important driving force that guides every organization, including our government. If you're a citizen, this is *your* country and the government works for *you*. Our Constitution mandates what purposes the government should fulfill for you. Only you can decide whether it has fulfilled these in the past and if it is fulfilling them today, and the likelihood that it will in the future based on how things have gone and are going. That's your call. You're on the board, you oversee it and it works for you. So take a minute, look at each of the purposes above and make your own decision about whether or not it is fulfilling its duty to you as mandated in our Constitution.

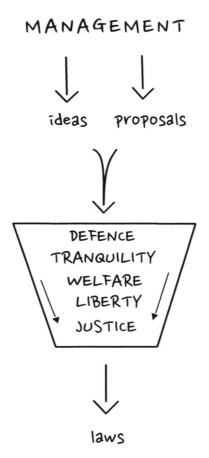

———— ——

"The care of human life and happiness and
not their destruction is the first and only
legitimate object of good government."

—Thomas Jefferson in a letter written to a group
of supporters on March 31, 1809, shortly after the
conclusion of his second term as president

————

CHAPTER 11

Management

WE KNOW THAT EVERY ORGANIZATION HAS some kind of purpose that guides its activity and focus. I think we can all agree with the purposes of our government, as laid out in our Constitution. What's much more difficult is organizing the government so that it can fulfill those purposes, and to do so in a way that will last far into the future.

This is where management comes in. These are the individuals—from only one person to millions, depending on the size of the organization—that structure and organize things in such a way that allows the purposes of the group to be accomplished. This is where the rubber meets the road. This is what makes a great company that thrives and lasts for decades, or even centuries.

First comes the initial idea. You might, for example, come up with a new kind of car paint that will change colors with the turn of a switch on the dashboard, giving drivers choices like they've never had before. A driver could select white on the way to work, green when going to lunch and black for a night out on the town. You've revolutionized car paint.

Now what do you do? How do you get it sold? How do you get it made in huge quantities? How do you pay for it all? This is when you build an organization that has the purpose to fabricate and sell your paint. Fulfilling that purpose becomes the organization's *job*. The organization soon is made up of sales and marketing people, managers, accountants, lawyers, chemists, shipping personnel, receptionists, executives, etc. They all get paid to fulfill the purpose of the company: to make and sell paint.

It's very important here to realize that the personnel running the organization are just as vital to its survival as the original idea that started the whole chain of events, and sometimes even more so! A great product or idea certainly won't sell itself. For example, how many great ideas for products or services have you had in your life? We've all had them! We see a way of doing something better and come up with a great solution, but that's as far as it goes. Not because the idea is bad, but because there's no organization that could profitably get it into the hands of those who could use it.

McDonald's is a great example of this. Taking beef, grinding it and making it into a patty was a nice idea. Putting it on bread and adding other good-tasting things like pickles, catsup and mustard was wise, too, because it helped the meat taste better. All good ideas, but not revolutionary. I think it's fair to estimate that, over the years, millions of restaurants have served hamburgers, many of them selling nothing but hamburgers. So why did McDonald's become the world's largest hamburger company instead of Wendy's or Burger King or Carl's Jr.? Why did McDonald's make it when so many other great hamburger restaurants didn't? Simply because McDonald's had smarter ideas about how to organize, all of which were developed by individuals— the management running the organization.

Any product or service, regardless of the quality of the idea, must have competent management creating a workable organization and system that gets its product or service to the end user. *Period.*

The bottom line is that management—the individuals who oversee the day-to-day functions of the organization—determines the success and longevity of an organization, or the failure and end of one.

Why did the bookstore chain Borders go out of business, and Barnes & Noble didn't? Why did Pan Am Airlines fail after sixty-four years in business, and United Airlines is still flying? Why did Circuit City fail, and Best Buy didn't? There is no other reason than one had better management than the other. Again, management isn't something that you can just buy; management is made up of skilled *individuals* working to achieve the purposes of the organization.

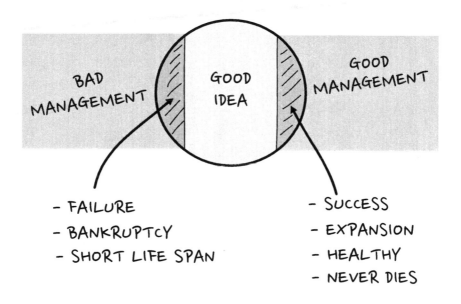

- FAILURE
- BANKRUPTCY
- SHORT LIFE SPAN

- SUCCESS
- EXPANSION
- HEALTHY
- NEVER DIES

If management runs the organization, then who oversees management? The board of directors—that's their job. Do the individuals on the board need to know how to manage the company? No, that's management's job. But it's *vital* that the individual board members know whether management is *doing* their job or not. And it's very important for them to know this *long* before things have gotten so bad that the company has to declare bankruptcy.

So how can a board member know whether the company is healthy, and if management is doing its job? *By looking to see whether the purposes of the organization are being achieved.* In the car paint business I mentioned above, a board member might look at the current sales volume of the organization to determine whether it's up or down. They might also look at the number of customer returns, which will indicate whether the quality control department is doing its job. Of course, the most important numbers they'll want to see are profit figures. Is the company making money, or not? Again, even if the company is a non-profit, it still *must* bring in more money than it spends. For example, the Red Cross must bring in more in donations than it spends to help people and run its organization, or it won't survive.

In the end, the board of directors must have a good grasp on the *health* of the organization in order to do its job. It must determine whether the organization is doing well and take action to ensure that success continues. Or, if the organization is doing poorly, how to get it doing well again. Both situations, good and bad, require action, but it is *especially* important in the second case. If the organization is doing poorly, the board must *act*, or the organization may just continue doing poorly and eventually end up *bankrupt*.

For example, if the company is going broke, the board has a number of options. They can talk to management to find out what's going on and make sure they (management) know that things must change. They can bring in a consultant to help advise them on what's wrong with the company. They can also fire management and bring in a new team to run the company. In fact, the board can continue firing and bringing in new management teams until one of the groups they hire finally fixes the problem. Remember, management is the *only* difference between many companies surviving or failing.

So how does this apply to our role as members of the board of directors over our government? In *exactly* the same way. We are members of the board that oversees our government. Our government is run by a management team, made up of the president and Congress. Our Constitution clearly lays out what our government is supposed to be delivering to us, as covered in the last chapter.

The only question to answer is whether the government, as directed by management, is fulfilling its duty to us—the people it serves.

"Here, sir, the people govern. Here they act by their immediate representatives."

—Alexander Hamilton during a debate on June 24, 1788, about whether the state of New York should ratify the Constitution (New York voted for ratification a month later)

CHAPTER 12

Is It or Isn't It?

To DO OUR JOB AS MEMBERS OF THE BOARD, we need to know whether or not our government is achieving its purpose. With that information, we can take the appropriate actions. So let's take another quick look at what our government is mandated to provide for us by our Constitution, which we covered in detail earlier in the book. The Constitution requires our government to:

1. Form a more perfect union

2. Establish justice

3. Ensure domestic tranquility

4. Provide for the common defense

5. Promote the general welfare

6. Secure the blessings of liberty for ourselves and posterity

First, we need to acknowledge the brilliance of the idea to allow the people of this country—its citizens—to oversee their government. This one idea, put into practice in our country in 1776, was new and brave and has changed the world forever.

Next, I think it's clear that up to this point, our Constitution has created a more perfect union than what existed under the Articles of Confederation and Perpetual Union. Our country and its citizens, taken as a whole over the last two centuries, have certainly prospered compared to most other countries. We've had arguably better justice than others around the world, and our country has been mostly tranquil and our states well protected. From a very long-term, 240-year view, management has done a very good job. Though it isn't perfect, it's unlikely that there is a better system of government anywhere in the world.

Okay, so that's the long-term, overall look at our government. But how is it doing today? Is management achieving its purposes for us in the present? This is critical information for us as board members, so we know what actions to take. The information must be factual, without bias or opinion. It must be simple to understand and easily accessible. And, most importantly, it needs to inform us as to whether the most vital and important purposes, those most critical to us and the health and survival of our country, are being achieved.

Obviously, there's no way we're all going to agree on all issues when it comes to our country. Everyone will have a different opinion about the current state of justice, freedom, safety, economic prosperity and the myriad of other issues that affect us all. We're all individuals and we're going to see things from our own perspective, so we may not all agree on whether our government is really doing its job to "promote the general welfare" for each of us.

This is where political parties come in, fighting to achieve our country's purposes on behalf of their membership. Democrats tend to want government-mandated health care, while Republicans don't. Republicans tend to not want any regulation on guns, whereas Democrats more commonly do. Then there are the differences regarding abortion, welfare, immigration, environmental protection, etc. The list goes on and on, and we probably will never all entirely agree on any of these issues.

But are there some issues that all of us—the entire board—*can* agree on? Well, it certainly doesn't seem like it. Everything we read in the press makes it look like one side is against the other—that the Democrat's view is against the Republican's view, or the Libertarian's ideas are conflicting with another party's ideas. In fact, it seems that conflict is *everywhere*.

There's good reason for that. In an earlier chapter, we talked about how we all love a good contest. It's in our nature to fight for something against something else. We live for the drama, the competition. It's part of our makeup, and it's what makes up life. So it makes sense for us to concentrate our attention on issues of conflict, right?

The other reason conflict seems to be everywhere? The press *exists* because of it. They learned long ago that any good news story has to contain conflict or it isn't of interest, and therefore won't result in sales and clicks. Why? Again, because we love conflict! So in order to get viewers and readers, the media provides us with stories of great conflicts so that we're eager to see what the latest score is and whether our side is winning or losing. If they can sprinkle a little sex and scandal into the story, all the better! So between our own love of drama and conflict, and the fact that we get most of our news from organizations that know this, it makes sense that we feel divided as a nation.

But the truth is, there are things we *can* and *do* agree on. They just don't come to mind because they aren't in the public conversation and they aren't a major point of conflict, and because we *agree* on them. We'll get to this soon, but first there are some other points we need to discuss.

Here is a key question that must be considered by all board members: Are all issues equally important to the survival of our country? It doesn't take much thinking on this to realize that no, they aren't. Does every issue equally impact our quality of life? Definitely not. Just like in our own lives, not every problem or difficulty is equal. The fact that our car might need a wash is not nearly as important as making sure our rent or mortgage is paid. Being able to buy food is far more critical than whether the government passes a law protecting a local river.

This is not to say that the various issues we all fight for are not important, because they are. But we also need to get the correct perspective from our positions as board members. It's our responsibility to ensure the *overall* well-being of our country as a whole first and foremost, and with that taken care of, we can then make decisions based on regional, local and even personal interests.

To get the right perspective on this, let's say our country is a giant ship sailing across a vast ocean. Would all problems or issues on the ship be equally important? Would a problem such as litter not being picked up on the decks be as important as a leak in the hull? Would equal health care for everyone on the ship be as important as a leak in the hull? Possibly, if the leak was extremely minor. But what if the leak wasn't small, and no one had any idea how to plug it up? And what if the water levels in the hull grew higher than ever before, to the point that it was unimaginable that it could ever be pumped out? It would quickly become obvious which issue was more important, because if the ship sinks, none of the other issues would matter. The ship must float, or it ceases to be a place on which to live.

As a member of the board of directors over the management and operation of the ship, wouldn't you insist that *any* issue affecting the ability of the ship to float be immediately and thoroughly handled? And what would your opinion be of anyone who tried to downplay the danger of the leak, and all the water that was building up in the hull? Would you sit by quietly and listen to them? Or would you disregard their misdirection and do your job to ensure that management repairs the hull, stops the leak and secures the proper pump to reduce the amount of water in the hull?

Now, what if management knew about the leak in the hull for a long time, like a year, and yet they let it continue to leak? What would your assessment be of the executives in charge of the ship at that point? Okay, let's go further with this. What if those executives had known about, and condoned, the leak for ten years? Would you think it was time for a new set of executives? Well, what if they'd let it go on for twenty years? Would it be time to replace them at that point? It's hard to imagine that any good management team of a ship would let a leak continue over such a long time, especially when it threatened the very survival of the ship and all those aboard. If this were a real scenario, with a real ship, the captain would be removed from his position and most likely face a prison sentence.

Let's take the scenario closer to home for a minute. What if your spouse continually spent more money than both of you were making, month after month, with your personal debt growing bigger and bigger? What would you do? What if he kept doing it even after you told him to stop? What if he continued this for ten years, and it got to the point where he had caused so much debt to pile up that you could *never* pay it off? At some point, wouldn't you divorce him and look for a new spouse?

So let's apply this to our country. Are there any issues or problems that are critical to its basic survival—issues we might consider more important than almost *all* other issues? How about these two: 1) Safety and 2) economic viability? Let's take a closer look at these.

SAFETY: Doesn't our own personal safety and that of our family and friends take precedence over anything else? If we were at war, with an enemy bombing our cities and marching across our land, wouldn't this absolutely be more important than *any* other issue? Would anything else besides winning that war and being safe occupy our attention? I think not. We instinctively understand that unless we're alive, nothing else happens, so any threat to our lives quickly becomes the center of our attention until that threat is alleviated. And if you're a parent, as I am, this extends to an even greater extent regarding any threat to your children.

I doubt that there is a more important issue than the overall safety of our country. And I don't mean safety from faraway threats, whether imagined or real—say in Iraq or Afghanistan. I'm talking about the safety of our physical country, our cities, water supplies, homes, schools and families, right here on our soil. This is one of the constitutional purposes of our government, to "provide for the common defence."

Is this an issue we need to argue over? Does anyone on the board feel that it would be a *good* thing for us to have an enemy invading us? Do we need to take a poll or see what the leaders of whatever political party we belong to have to say about this? No. Is this one issue everyone on the board can agree on? I think so.

ECONOMIC VIABILITY: "Viability" comes from an old word meaning "life." It means "capable of living."[1] Used in this sense, "economic viability" would simply mean "something able to live and survive financially."

Would this be important to our country, to be able to survive financially? Without a question. Even though our country isn't a business or corporation, the rules of bringing in more money than is spent still applies. If our country were in a bad financial condition—constantly spending more than it brings in and growing debt—wouldn't this affect us all? Wouldn't it be more ideal if our country had ample reserves and plenty of money to ensure that we're all well cared for and happy and that we can defend ourselves and build roads and other infrastructure? In our own lives, if we have too much debt and can't pay back what we owe, we have big problems. I know it may not seem like it, but this applies to our country as well, even though it hasn't caught up to us yet. Also, in the eyes of our enemies, we only look weaker if we're overloaded with debt. We'd be seen as much stronger if we had no debt and massive reserves in the bank.

Isn't this also an issue we can all agree on? Would anyone—except someone who wished the United States harm—want our country to be anything but incredibly strong economically? I think not. But it's not always easy to tell if the actions of our government are causing economic strength or not, so let's look at this one a little closer.

---

[1] Merriam-Webster Dictionary.

Per our Constitution, our government has the purpose to "promote the general welfare." Does a government that spends in such a way that results in massive debt, and continues overspending year after year, fulfill that purpose? Our government currently has over $18 trillion in debt, so much money that it's almost impossible to conceive of.

You've probably heard many comparisons before, like how a trillion dollar bills stacked up would reach a height of 68,000 miles, more than 10,000 times higher than a jet flies. Or that a trillion *seconds* is equal to 32,000 *years*. How much is a trillion grains of sand? Enough to fill 150 dump trucks! It's a number so big, it seems mythical. But it's real, and when multiplied by eighteen, it's the amount of money our government—the one we're in charge of, that works for us—*owes*.

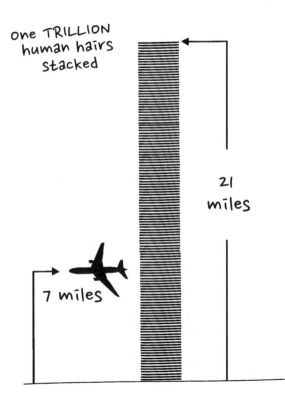

One TRILLION human hairs stacked

21 miles

7 miles

It's important to realize that this amount of debt didn't happen overnight, or by some fluke, or just by our government overspending a couple of times. Remember, our government is managed by *real* people—*citizens* of our country. I remind you of this because it can be easy to think of Congress or the government as a thing, or a machine. But it's composed of people—people who make decisions. Decisions that, in hindsight, may have looked brilliant at the time, but seem less so now that we have more debt than we can ever realistically pay off.

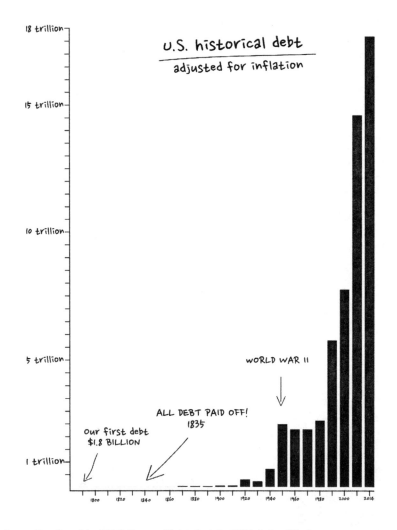

Sources: Data from Sahr (2015); Bureau of Labor Statistics CPI Inflation Calculator.

How did we get all that debt? Simply by spending more money than the government brought in. That's where a budget comes in. You predict that a certain amount of money is going to come in, and plan to spend it on the various things needed. You can't spend more than you bring in, or you have a deficit. Having a deficit means you have to borrow to pay for the extra expenses not covered by the money that came in. Borrowing, of course, leads to debt, and in the case of our government, that debt is now $18 trillion.

The real question is: How could our debt have grown to such enormous heights? By overspending, of course—by having a deficit. But in the case of our government, it didn't happen overnight. We haven't just had a deficit once or twice, or even ten or twenty times. We've had a deficit seventy-two times in the last eighty-four years! That's right. According to the U.S. Treasury, our government has spent more money than it had in *seventy-two* of the last eighty-four years—since 1931.[2]

If you need to take a moment to re-read that last sentence, I understand. Like the enormity of our debt, it's hard to comprehend. Only twelve times in the last eighty-four years, our government did *not* overspend and had that rare and unheard-of condition called a *surplus*. Only twelve times out of eighty-four, our government spent *less* than it had available to spend.

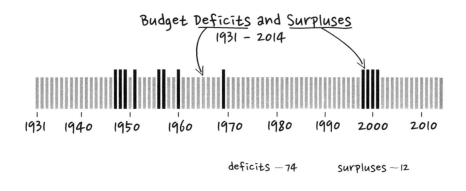

deficits — 74   surpluses — 12

---

[2] White House Office of Management and Budget, "Historical Tables."

And unfortunately, unless something changes, that dismal track record isn't going to improve any time soon: our government's budget analysts predict that we'll have a deficit *every* year for the next ten years, which is as far out as they can comfortably predict. In fact, they predict that our deficit will hold steady at around $450 billion a year for the next few years and then start increasing until 2025, when they estimate it will hit a trillion dollars—a *year!* [3]

Remember, this is the amount our own government predicts it will *overspend* every year. This is the amount they expect to have to borrow every year to pay for everything they authorize. This is the amount of money yearly that will be *added* to our overall national debt—the amount we owe, the amount we've borrowed and *the amount the next generation will inherit.*

I know this doesn't seem possible or comprehensible. It's so incomprehensible and so hard to grasp, in fact, that we don't do anything about it. It doesn't make sense. It seems to violate the laws of money and math. You can't just keep spending more than you bring in *forever*. If you or I did this for very long, we'd be bankrupt. Any company that did this would be out of business.

No, there aren't any special rules for governments that say they can take on as much debt as they want for as long as they want without having to pay it back. They might be able to ignore it longer than you or I could, but someone at some point is going to have to live with the consequences of so much debt, especially if it continues to grow. And if it doesn't adversely affect you or me in our lifetimes, it certainly *will* affect those Americans who come after us—our children, and their children.

In the end, the truth is that the responsibility to do something about our government's overspending falls on you, me and the other citizens of our country who oversee our government. We're our country's board

---

[3] Congressional Budget Office, "The Budget and Economic Outlook: 2015 to 2025."

of directors, so it's up to us to make the changes—drastic ones, if necessary—to ensure that the leak in our ship gets plugged, and that we stop spending more than we have and stop adding to our debt. It's up to us, and no one but us, because *no one else has the power* to ensure that our country is strong and healthy for us and the future generations of Americans.

So I ask you this: Do you think the management team currently in charge of our government is fulfilling its purpose to promote the general welfare for us all, as laid out by the Constitution, based on their record of managing the financial affairs of our government? That's for you to decide so you can act accordingly—one way or the other—from your position on the board.

"Blessed are the young, for they shall inherit the national debt."

—Former president Herbert Hoover making a sarcastic point in a speech on January 16, 1936

CHAPTER 13

what's the Problem with a Little Debt?

Our country's debt seems to grow and get bigger without affecting us in any way. Seemingly (and almost literally) every year our government overspends and our national debt grows, but the country keeps going. We have yet to see any bankruptcy proceedings against our treasury department. No one has imposed an extra tax on food that is a "pay down the debt" tax, so it's difficult to see what the big deal is about having national debt. In fact, it pretty much seems like the government can just spend as much as it wants without any consequences. But let's not forget—it's much easier to *go into* debt than it is to *get out* of it.

Look, there's nothing wrong with debt itself. Most people would never be able to buy a house or car without it. The trick is making sure you can cover the payments. As you take on more debt, the payments increase and take up more and more of the income you need to cover expenses like food, gas, mortgage, rent, insurance, utilities and other basic needs. If you have enough money coming in, covering your debt payments can be easy. But it's an entirely different story if your payments continue to rise or your income drops, and you've already cut out all unnecessary purchases yet you still don't have enough to cover everything.

It's at this point that hard choices have to be made about what *not* to buy. Do you buy less food? Do you skip paying your mortgage or rent? Do you cut back on using your car to save on gas? Or should you skip paying for auto insurance? Unless you make more money, or figure out a way to cut expenses, you've got a massive problem. Bankruptcy is one of the ways people solve this problem, but that comes with its own problems:

1. It ruins your credit for at least seven to ten years.

2. You'll have to pay a higher interest rate to borrow money in the future because you've proven quite clearly that you don't always pay back what you borrow, so you're a higher risk to anyone who might lend you money.

3. The person or organization you owe may not get fully paid back, so now they're out of the money you promised to pay them back. You broke a promise to repay the person or organization that lent you the money, which doesn't help one's general self-respect.

The *same* rules apply to a government. But governments that print their own money, like ours, can get away with taking on debt for much longer than you or I could. It can only do this for so long, however, before the dollar starts losing its value. Printing money to pay back debt is a short-term solution. The minimal long-term solution is to stop increasing the debt and, ideally, start paying it off.

It's our duty as members of our country's board of directors to understand the basic finances of *our* government. We can't put the blame on anyone else because we—and only we—have the final say in who runs our country. We are the only ones who can change management.

As stated earlier, the U.S. is currently in debt to the tune of $18 trillion, which is owed to China, Japan, Brazil and a slew of other countries that have lent us money. We also owe the Social Security and Medicare funds. You may have money invested in a mutual fund that lent money to our government. If you have any money in U.S. government bonds, you've lent money to our government.[1]

The problem isn't necessarily the amount we owe; it's the *size* of the payments on that debt. Regarding the $18 trillion debt, at the time of this writing our Treasury Department reports that we're paying about $633 million a day in *interest alone* ($231 billion a year).[2] That's $633 million a *day*, every day of the year, on interest, that buys us nothing and doesn't pay down the debt at all.

As a comparison, our country spends about $386 million per day on education ($141 billion a year).[3] Our government spends 1.6 times as much on its debt's *interest payments* than it does on education for our children. Obviously this is not good. But we took on the debt, so we need to make the payments.

Another factor we need to understand is that the interest rate on our debt is currently historically low. The exact rate fluctuates, but it's been around or below two percent.[4] Of course, the interest rate is what helps determine our payment, so if the interest rate is low, our payment is low. As the interest rate goes up, so does the amount of our payment. This works the same for the government as it does for you and me.

And interest rates *will* go up, without a doubt, for two reasons: 1) the rates are historically low right now and won't stay there forever and 2) interest rates are determined by risk. If there's a very low risk of losing money in an investment, the interest rate will be low. Naturally, if there's a high risk of losing money, the rate will be high. Our government is currently paying so little interest on its debt because people trust that the U.S. government will always pay them back. But as we take on more and more debt, investors may consider us a more *risky* investment, and thus require a higher interest rate to

[1] Bui, "Everyone the U.S. Government Owes Money To, In One Graph."
[2] Edelberg, "CBO's Projection of Federal Interest Payments."
[3] New America Foundation, "The Federal Education Budget."
[4] Edelberg, "CBO's Projection of Federal Interest Payments."

compensate for that risk. And if investors feel that lending money
to our government is a bit risky, they won't do it—unless they get a
higher rate of interest to compensate them for the extra risk on the
investment.

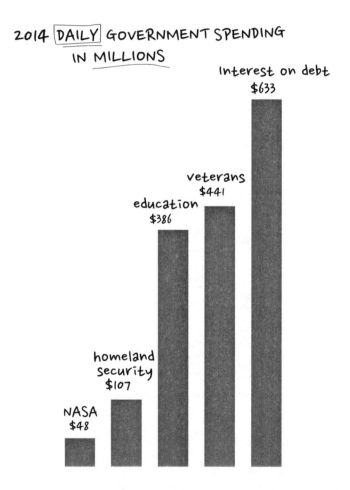

2014 DAILY GOVERNMENT SPENDING
IN MILLIONS

Interest on debt
$633

veterans
$441

education
$386

homeland
security
$107

NASA
$48

Sources: Data from Edelberg (2014); United States Department of Veterans Affairs (2015);
New America (2015); Congressional Research Service (2014); NASA (2015).

Let's say our government continues to pile on debt so that investors get nervous and won't lend us the amount we need to cover our overspending and debt payments, unless they get four percent interest on the money they lend us.[5] Four percent is still a very low interest rate, but it would be double the rate we're currently paying. Then our payment on the $18 trillion would also double, bringing it up to around $1.2 billion a *day* ($462 billion a year). At the time of this writing, the government projects that by 2024 we'll be paying $2.1 billion a day ($800 billion a year) in interest alone.[6]

As our debt payment grows larger, the government will either need to a) bring in more income, b) borrow more money or c) cut back on other spending. The normal course of action for our government is to just borrow more money to cover its debt payment and everything else in the budget. But increased borrowing then means a higher debt payment. The more debt we take on, the riskier it will be for investors to lend us money, so we'll need to raise the interest rate to compensate for their extra risk. And a higher rate of interest then means a larger interest payment.

Eventually, we will not be able to keep borrowing to cover our country's bills. At some point, we're going to have to scale back our spending to meet the amount of money we have to spend. And when that happens, the size of our debt payment will restrict the amount of money we can spend on other budget items. Something will have to be cut back or go unpaid.

Should we just not pay the interest we owe to those we've borrowed from? Doing that would be disastrous, since people, organizations and governments around the world that rely on that income would be thrown into turmoil. That would throw the world economy into disarray, hurting us all dramatically. Not to mention that if we did that,

---

[5] Edelberg, "CBO's Projection of Federal Interest Payments."

[6] Ibid.

we would be demonstrating that we're a risky investment, and investors would therefore demand an even *higher* interest rate. This means our debt payments would go up even more, and then we'd have even less money for other budget items.

So we definitely *don't* want to miss making any payments to those we owe money to. But *something* has to be cut back. Do we cut back on Social Security payments, or Medicare? Do we cut back on the funding for our military, or education? Maybe we should slash NASA's budget and scrap our space program. How about closing our national parks to save some budget money? In order to balance the budget and not borrow more, something would have to be cut back.

If all that isn't bad enough, there's still one more part of this we need to understand. Not only do we have a debt so big that it's almost impossible to imagine, and not only do we currently pay $633 million a day in interest payments alone on that debt, but every year our government *continues* to overspend which just adds more to the debt!

Are you still with me? If you're thinking that this all seems unbelievable, you're right—it is *unbelievable*. It's so unbelievable that we don't do anything about it. But unbelievable or not, it's the situation we're in, it's real, it's happening now and believe me, the consequences will be very real if we don't jump on it now while we're still able to do something about it.

It isn't too late. We haven't reached the point of no return. With smart action, we can turn this around for our country. But it's up to us to put the right management in place—one that will stop adding to our debt. We're the board of directors. We have the power. Now we need to use that power, and press our country's reset button to put us back on the right track.

"I am not among those who fear the people. They, and not the rich, are our dependence for continued freedom. And to preserve their independence, we must not let our rulers load us with perpetual debt."

—Thomas Jefferson in a letter to a local
resident written on July 12, 1816

CHAPTER 14

We Are Them, They Are Us

BEFORE WE GO ANY FURTHER, WE HAVE TO CLEAR something up about the elected leaders who make up the management team we put in place to oversee our government. One of our guiding principles along our journey to finding the reset button is looking for pieces of truth. There's a great deal that obscures our view of what's going on with our government, and whenever we can cut through the fog to see some reality, we need to do it. And this is one of those opportunities.

A national survey by Rasmussen Reports recently found that only sixteen percent of us think that the management we have in place over our government is doing a good or excellent job.[1] This implies that eighty-four percent are dissatisfied in some way. (Just as a side note here—if eighty-four percent of the shareholders of any company in America were dissatisfied with the management team overseeing the operation of the organization they owned stock in, I think there would be a hundred percent chance that those managers would be out of a job.) Rasmussen also found that only thirty-two percent of us think our country is headed in the right direction.[2]

It's certainly nothing new that people are dissatisfied with their elected leaders. But if you've ever heard people talk about the government and how bad it is, you commonly hear them use the word "they." "*They*

---

[1] Rasmussen Reports, "Congressional Performance."
[2] Ibid., "Right Direction or Wrong Track."

don't know what they're doing." "*They're* a bunch of crooks." "*They've* ruined this country." "*They* need to be thrown out!"

Source: Data from Rasmussen Reports (2015).

Whenever anyone tells me that "they" did this or that, if it isn't clear to me who that person is talking about in the context of the conversation, I make sure I find out who "they" is. It's way too easy, especially in an argument, for a person to start throwing "they" around. What I often find is "they" turns out to be just one or two or a handful of people. "They" is hard to conceive of because the word doesn't specify anyone in particular.

The truth is that *individuals* cause things to happen, not "they." And individuals within groups, whether they're acting together or alone, cause any and all actions to occur. A group isn't a living entity in itself. It can't think or do anything, as it isn't a living being. But when people within a group, acting as a group, do something, we commonly think of the group as the "they" that has done that action.

When we're talking about our government, we need to understand that Congress is a group made up of *individuals*. Those individuals are human, just like us. They get up in the morning, just like you and me. They come from different parts of the country. They are men and women of various religions and ethnicities. They probably knew few, if any, other members of Congress when they got elected. They each have campaign contributors (the reality of our system) and voters from their home district that they need to please. Many have wives, husbands and children to think about. To get elected, they must: 1) be a citizen of our country, 2) be a resident in the district or area they are elected to represent and 3) be at least thirty years old to be a senator or twenty-five years old to be a member of the House of Representatives. And, of course, we hope that they also have a desire to do right by our country. But in the end, the members of Congress are a very diverse group of *individuals*.

Yes, it's easy to think of them as "they." Yes, these individuals we elect to Congress tend to form smaller groups, whether by party, race, special interests or other categories. And we generally just lump them all together and think of them as one body called "Congress." When the country isn't doing well, it's easy and convenient to blame them, as a whole.

Now, it may seem like I'm trying to let them off the hook. I'm not in the slightest, as you'll see in a future chapter. My point is that the road to finding and pushing our country's reset button includes understanding more deeply what is at the heart of the problem. We need to push past what everyone simply accepts as truth and give it closer inspection. We need to push past the simple notion that "they"—Congress as a whole—are destroying our country, because we've been blaming our problems on Congress for a long time and it's gotten us nowhere. Blaming them hasn't solved the problem!

It's important for us to understand that Congress is made up of individuals. That's all. It isn't some big, unknown, all-powerful group that we can't do anything about.

There's another aspect to the subject of "they" that we must understand, which is this: *they* are really *us*. It's so easy for problems to be blamed on someone else. And sometimes it's true—sometimes there is someone else to blame. But in this case, there really isn't. If the people who made up Congress were from some other country and were put in power without our approval, then we might be able to stand back with our arms folded and say, "*They* are hurting our country."

But that isn't the case in this situation. The people who make up Congress are citizens of the U.S., *just like we are*. The people who run for Congress must, by law, *be one of us*. One of us decides to run, we vote them in, they spend at least two years in office and then someone else—another one of us—runs against them and wins or loses, and the cycle continues. And even when they're a member of Congress, they are still *one of us*. Every new person going into Congress is *one of us*. Every person in Congress is *one of us*. They *are* us!

And as long as we're on such a hunt for truth, there's another harsh reality we must acknowledge: *We* put them there! *We* voted them in. And—I hate to bring this up, but I think it's unavoidable at this juncture—if Congress isn't doing the job we want and we're dissatisfied, who's ultimately responsible for that? We're the only ones who have the power to put them there, or to kick them out, so unfortunately (or fortunately, really) it's on us. Personally, I'd rather have this responsibility, because it means that we *can* do something about it. It would be *much* worse if we didn't have the power to change what goes on in our government. This point is vital to understanding the reset button.

We give our elected representatives their authority and power to run our government. They are us, and we give them their power.

I know, the reality of all this can be a bit harsh. But believe me, it's incredibly vital to finding the reset button. So don't lose heart, don't think that all is hopeless. We're getting very close to our goal of finding a way to easily make sweeping change in our government.

"If you could kick the person in the pants responsible for most of your trouble, you wouldn't sit for a month."

—President Theodore Roosevelt

CHAPTER 15

Broken System

NOW THAT WE'VE DETERMINED THAT "THEY" are actually us, we'd better come to grips with what many of us regularly say about us: "Politicians are a bunch of crooks." "They're just a bunch of liars!" "They only care about enriching themselves." And countless more accusations. Most statements like this start with "they" and end with something very derogatory.

Well, if *they* are *us*, then according to those statements, we're *all* a bunch of crooks. Though some may think that mankind is generally evil and needs to be controlled and tamed, I do not. I think the innate nature of man is good. I believe that, deep down, people want to improve their lives and the lives of others and prosper. Are there bad people who are bent on destruction? Absolutely, and we all need to stay alert for them. But I think that the majority of people—almost all, in fact—are good, decent and caring to a greater or lesser degree, depending on the immediate circumstances.

I also think that this applies to politicians. As I mentioned earlier, I grew up around them. I briefly worked for a U.S. senator. In the non-profit I started, I work to get privacy legislation passed and as part of that, I interact with elected officials. Many, if not most, of the politicians I've known personally have been good, decent people.

Unfortunately, we always hear about the few bad ones, the ones who really are crooks, who are there for their own enrichment and power and not to help us. Those few, when caught, are talked about endlessly in the press. They become a big deal. And it's so easy and convenient to then equate that one bad individual with *all* politicians. Things are going bad in the government, the press shows us a bad politician, and we decide that they must all be bad—end of story.

Take a look at your own thoughts on this for a moment. Do you think all politicians are crooks? That they're all bad? That they're only in it for themselves? That they're just power-hungry?

But is that *really* true? Are they *all* that way? Even if you've never personally met or known a politician, are you able to find any examples of what you consider to be a good politician? What about President Kennedy? Was he working for the good of the country? Or President Lincoln? He was a politician. Was he a crook, too?

My point is that it's very important for us to spot and reconsider some of these "truths" that get thrown around in our country about our government. Though they may sound good and make it easier for us to blame someone else, it's important that we be honest with ourselves and determine whether they're actually true. And the truth is, this one is *not* true. There *are* good politicians. Remember, truth leads us to answers. False information leads us to poor solutions.

So if it's not true that everyone elected to Congress is a crook, then what's going on? If they *were* all crooks, it would be easy to fix the problem. But that isn't the case. So what *is* the problem?

Well, here's another truth that we need to understand. There can be any number of answers to a problem, but only one of those answers will be the best one. And the best one can only be determined *if it fixes the problem*. If it doesn't fix the problem, it's the wrong answer. The trick, though, is finding the answer that fixes the problem!

In the case of our country, I think we can all agree that it certainly seems like our politicians aren't acting in our best interest. We all have our points of view on what we don't like about our government, but I think we can all agree that being $18 trillion in debt isn't good for the long-term health of our country. So let's name the problem: our elected leaders are not representing us, the people who put them there, in a way that best benefits our country. Does that about sum it up?

So what's the solution? That's the trick, isn't it? Naming the problem is pretty easy, but finding the answer may not be. It isn't that we can't come up with a lot of different solutions or answers. People and organizations around the country work on implementing solutions to fix this problem every day.

I have a solution, too, and while it may or may not be the very best one, I believe it will lead to a greatly improved overall performance of our elected leaders. More on that just a bit later.

First, let's step into the shoes of someone who decides that he or she wants to do something to help the country, and let's walk in their shoes to get a better idea of the journey they take. Let's assume, for this scenario, that the person is not a crook, but actually wants to help. Let's see what happens to them that might cause them to act in a way that fits our general consensus regarding the behavior of politicians.

Let's call this made-up person Silvia Jones. Silvia doesn't like what Congress is doing and wants to do her duty as a citizen to try and improve it. So she decides to run for a seat in the House of Representatives. In her research, she reads an article reporting that, in the 2012 elections, those who won seats in the House spent an average of $1.5 million on their election campaigns.[1] That's far more than Silvia has, so she decides she'll do what almost every other politician does—she'll ask people for campaign donations. She starts holding rallies and gives speeches to spread her ideas, telling the people that she'll represent them honestly and improve the country.

People like what she has to say, and those in her district start giving her money. Some people give her $25, others $50. But there are others who give her $2,700, the maximum amount anyone can give directly to one politician. Word spreads around the country about Silvia and her ideas, and she starts receiving $2,700 checks from people around the

---

[1] Choma, "Election 2012: The Big Picture Shows Record Cost of Winning a Seat in Congress."

country, outside her district. Then she meets a man who represents a large association of businesses, and he lets her know that she's going to start receiving lots of checks from the workers in those businesses. And then one day, she meets a really wealthy man who gives her $2,700, just like the others. But he doesn't stop there. He tells her that he likes her ideas so much, he's going to give $42,000 to her party, which is totally legal. On top of all of this, he thinks she's so amazing that he's going to spend $10 million of his own money running ads on TV, ensuring that everyone knows how great she is.

Silvia isn't sure why, but she doesn't feel too comfortable about all of this. Like most people, she doesn't like the feeling of being indebted to anyone. But she takes the money and is grateful for the help. She wins the election, rents an apartment in Washington D.C. and begins her new job as a congresswoman in the House of Representatives of the United States of America!

Silvia's made it. She's achieved her dream. She's now Congresswoman Jones. She starts looking over the various bills that are being debated and that she'll need to vote on. Phone calls start coming in from people who donated to her campaign, encouraging her to vote this way or that way on a bill. The rich man who spent so much to get her elected pays her a visit and tells her he needs her to vote "no" on a particular piece of legislation, and that it's *very* important to him. At this point, she's been on the job a whole week.

A few weeks later, she's having lunch with another member of the House who asks her how much money she's raised for her campaign. Silvia replies that she raised $2 million to win her election, which was just a few months ago. Her new friend clarifies her question: "How much have you raised this month for your *next* campaign?" Silvia gives her a blank look. So her friend continues: "Your next election is less than two years away. If it takes at least $1.5 million to win and keep your House seat, you need to be raising $60,000 *every* month from here on out."

Silvia sits in shock for a minute. She *just* finished campaigning, fundraising and running for office. She's been elected, and she just wants to work at being the best congresswoman she can be. But reality sets in, and she realizes that her next election isn't far away and she'll need a great deal of money to fight off someone else who will be after her job.

So what does Silvia do to raise all this money every month? She goes right back to the same people who gave her money before, and asks if they'll give again. Only this time, many of them ask how she's going to vote on this or that legislation. When she calls the rich guy to ask for money, he asks what her vote will be on that one bill he wanted her to vote "no" on.

Do you see where this is going? Can you see where things start going off track? Might this explain why our representatives act the way they do, once elected? The scenario above is very real. Each member of the House of Representatives is up for re-election every two years; each senator is up for re-election every six years.

The numbers in this example are accurate. In 2013, the Center for Responsive Politics reported that those who won seats in the House spent an average of $1.5 million on their campaigns, and those who won Senate seats each spent an average of $10 million.[2] This means that, on average, a member of the House needs to raise $60,000 per month, *every* month they're in office, to reach the $1.5 million mark for their next election. And this applies to *every* member of the House of Representatives! Senators need to raise an average of $140,000 every month. Every single senator! Every month, for six years! Some will raise more, some less.[3] Elizabeth Warren, for example, raised $42 million to win her Senate seat in 2012![4]

If these people we elect to be our representatives in Washington want to stay in office, they need to work at raising money *all* the time.

---

[2] Ibid.

[3] Ibid.

[4] Levenson, "After Her Record Haul, Warren Slips Into Red."

So if a particular politician gets a lot of campaign donations from, say, the oil industry, what should they do when a bill comes up for a vote that negatively affects that industry? What if they personally believe that the best decision for the country is to vote "no" on it? Should they risk losing all those campaign donations that they'll need for their next election?

But here's another angle on campaign fundraising that seldom gets talked about: instead of the donor telling the elected official how to vote, the elected official tells the potential donor that unless a donation is made, an upcoming vote won't go the way they like. It's been reported that this is done primarily by those elected officials who hold important positions in Congress that give them extensive power over votes and legislation.

For example, if you're the CEO of AT&T and a piece of legislation is moving through Congress that could cost your company hundreds of millions of dollars in new taxes, you of course want it to fail. Before long, you're contacted by a congressman who has the power to not allow the bill to come up for a vote (which would kill it), and tells you he's thinking of doing just that but isn't sure if you and the other companies affected by the bill really would like it to go away. What is that congressman telling you? He's saying that if you want the bill to go away, pay up. Do you take the risk of not making the donation? Or do you not only make the donation, but ensure that many of your employees do, too?

Does this actually happen? Many CEOs are speaking out that it does.[5] But doesn't it make sense that this type of activity does occur? The elected officials need money to run in their next election, and ultimately they have the power to make things happen that will help or hurt individuals and companies.

Money is vitally important to our elected officials. Maybe that's why

---

[5] Schweizer, Extortion: How Politicians Extract Your Money, Buy Votes, and Line Their Own Pockets.

it's so easy for us to equate them with crooks. But the way our system is set up, they *need* the money in order to fight to stay in their jobs every two or six years. It wouldn't be possible to be a successful politician without having money to spend.

Here's an example of how far this can go. In the 2012 national elections, it was reported that one individual, Sheldon Adelson, contributed $150 million in political donations and other spending on the election, primarily in favor of Republicans.[6] Understanding the incredible need politicians have for money in order to survive, does it seem right to you for one individual to give that much to influence our elections? Even Adelson himself doesn't necessarily think it's right, according to this quote attributed to him by *Forbes* magazine: "I'm against very wealthy people attempting to or influencing elections, but as long as it's doable, I'm going to do it."[7]

Even the most ethical and honest politician would have an incredibly difficult time not giving at least some sort of favoritism to those who donate money to their campaigns. It's human nature to want to repay someone for helping you. And our system puts our elected leaders in a situation where they constantly *need* to keep the money flowing in to fund their campaigns and keep their jobs. The system is set up so our elected officials are constantly having to chase money.

I believe that there are a lot of Silvias running for Congress, people who are generally very well-intended and want to help our country. I believe that they go in determined not to be corrupted or influenced by the power they'll have, or care about the money they'll need for their next election. But I also believe that the system is broken. It forces our representatives to pay too much attention to the interests of those who give them money, instead of paying full attention to the best interests of our country as a whole.

[6] Stone, "Sheldon Adelson Spent Far More On Campaign Than Previously Known."
[7] Bertoni, "Billionaire Sheldon Adelson Says He Might Give $100M to Newt Gingrich or Other Republican."

Does this mean that they're selling their votes? It's incredibly difficult to know for sure, but I believe that, in general, they don't. But let me ask you this: Outside of the small donations people make to help a candidate they believe in, why would anyone give large amounts of money if they didn't believe they'd be getting something back?

Can we go so far as to say a political donation tends toward a legal form of bribery? "Bribery" is defined as: "Money or some other benefit given to a person in power, especially a public official, in an effort to cause the person to take a particular action."[8]

True, when you make a political donation you don't tell the candidate which way to vote. But when a particular bill is up for a vote, do you let it be known how you want the official to vote? And if you then tell them that they need to vote for or against that bill, aren't you hoping they remember you gave them money for their election? And that you might give them more, or not? Well, what if you make a campaign donation and at the same time tell them to vote this way or that way on a bill? Can you legally do that? Absolutely. Does it mean every campaign donation is an act of bribery? Certainly not. But there's no doubt that money is needed by politicians to win elections, and it naturally follows that they'd be wise to pay close attention to those who give them money.

The bottom line is this: the system we've allowed to operate, in which our elected officials have to raise huge amounts of money just to stay in office, is deeply flawed. I believe it's the first and most important aspect of our government that needs to be fixed after we press the reset button. If we can take that massive influence over our elected representatives out of the equation, odds are very good that the decisions made in Washington D.C. would be better for our country as a whole.

One of the fundamental problems with the campaign fundraising system is that donations aren't limited to only those residing in a certain area related to the candidate. Any American citizen can donate to any

---

[8] American Heritage Dictionary.

political candidate running for any office anywhere in the country. So if I'm from Texas, I can donate to the campaign of a person running for Congress in Maine.

This happens all the time. During every election, the parties look over the states and determine the Congressional races in which they might be able to un-seat the other party. Then they routinely pour a tremendous amount of money into that one election to try to get the outcome in their favor. The theory is that if they pour enough money into that area to influence local voters to vote the way they want them to, then it will be money well spent and their candidate will have a better chance of winning. So in a sparsely populated state like Maine, millions of dollars might pour in from outside the state to affect that local election.

Why not have a law that restricts politicians from accepting a campaign donation from anyone living outside the district they're running in? That would give the elected candidate all the more reason to pay attention to those from his or her district because 1) they voted them in (and can vote them out) and 2) they're the only ones who can donate to support their next campaign.

Another idea: What if our elected officials had no idea who donated to their campaigns? Let's say we set up a system where all campaign donations went through a specific non-profit organization set up for this exact purpose. A person who wants to support Silvia Jones's election campaign writes a check to the non-profit indicating whose election fund they'd like the money to go to, and the non-profit then gives the money to Silvia's campaign without letting anyone connected to Silvia know who donated the money. In the end, the candidate would have no idea who specifically made donations to their campaign. They wouldn't feel obligated to give special attention to, or repay, *anyone*. They could focus their attention on doing the best job they could do for the voters who put them in office.

Can't you just sense how different it would be if this type of system were established? Do you think large donors would make those sizable contributions if the candidate never knew how much they gave? Probably not. The politician might raise less money in the end, but he or she wouldn't have to worry about paying back favors, and we'd have the management of our country better focused on making the best decisions for our country as a whole.

I certainly don't claim to be the first person to recognize that money is a problem in politics. The solutions I'm proposing are ideas that I think would work, but there are very smart people in our country with brilliant ideas to fix our campaign finance laws, and we'll definitely need them and their ideas to help straighten out this area once we've pressed the reset button. Many attempts have been made over the decades to get these kinds of laws implemented, but most have been largely unsuccessful.

And isn't it easy to see why? This type of legislation would be very unpopular to any individuals or organizations that donate large sums of money to our politicians. Unfortunately, some of the laws that used to help limit the amount that could be donated and spent on an election were recently struck down as unconstitutional by our Supreme Court. In two of the more recent decisions made by the Supreme Court, five of the judges said the laws were unconstitutional, while four said they weren't—a very close vote.[9]

So if all else fails and even the Supreme Court won't let us have laws that restrict campaign donations and the flow of money to our elected leaders, what do we do? We can always change the very document that instructs the Supreme Court—our country's Constitution, the same document that gives us the power to do just that. We're the only ones with that power. Though it hasn't been easy to do in the past, after we've pressed the reset button it might become much easier to accomplish—another positive reason to push it.

---

[9] Bravin, "Supreme Court Ends Overall Limit on Political Donations."

———————————

"All contributions by corporations to any
political committee or for any political
purpose should be forbidden by law."

—President Theodore Roosevelt in his State of the
Union address on December 5, 1905

———————————

CHAPTER 16

The Hidden War

NOW THAT WE UNDERSTAND OUR ROLE OVER our government better, we need to consider what possible role our enemies play in all of this.

Throughout history, people have been battling each other with advancing weaponry to win land, resources, energy and a million other things. Entire races have been displaced through war, only to move to another region of earth and then displace another race or culture. Since 1990 alone, we've fought the Persian Gulf War and the Iraq War, and we continue to fight the War in Afghanistan (and we've been drawn back into Iraq). The struggle amongst mankind for greater control and territory has been happening since the beginning.

We mainly use the term "war" when it's out in the open, utilizing aircraft, ships and other military weapons, including humans. But just because we don't see weapons and we aren't dodging bullets doesn't mean our enemies aren't pressing down on us. It's the hidden or invisible war that can be the most destructive, because it can catch you off guard and easily penetrate when you think all is quiet and safe.

We can't ignore the fact that there are those who would like us to fall from power. We are the most powerful nation in the world, we have our military staged strategically around the globe and we aren't shy about pressing our agenda when we think it's necessary. Whether we're right or wrong when we take action against a foreign country, it understandably creates hostility, and those we fight against would certainly like for us to become less powerful, if not altogether gone.

Other nations are advancing and becoming more important in the world theater and most, if not all of them, would probably like to overtake us as the most powerful nation in the world, whether that is a realistic position for them to achieve or not. There's a constant struggle amongst the leading and upcoming nations of the world for control, resources, territory and importance.

There are also various groups that operate independent of any recognized nation, with membership made up of an array of nationalities. Al-Qaeda is of course one such group that we've all heard of, and more recently ISIS, but there are more. Not all are bent on destroying us militarily, but many certainly have the aim of reducing our influence in the world.

Additionally, many individuals, the citizens of other countries, look upon us with all of our wealth, land, resources, opportunity and even movie stars with great envy. We've all felt how they feel—someone we know gets a great new job when we hate ours, or a friend finds the man or woman of their dreams, or a relative we don't really like strikes it rich. As much as we hate to admit it, sometimes we as humans hate the successes that others achieve. When you're the toughest on the block, people might act nice to you on the surface, but inside secretly wish for your failure.

There are also those U.S. citizens who, for various "reasons," work against their own country either directly or intentionally, or out of selfishness. The intentional types are usually associated with criminal acts against our government, like blowing up a truck in front of a courthouse, sending destructive devices or inhalants through the mail or hacking the computer networks of a government agency. The other type, those who are just selfish, are far less visible but dangerous nonetheless. They look and act just like you and me, but fail to realize that they are part of the larger group called Americans. They work to enrich themselves at the expense of us all. They create financial products that make them millions but ultimately spoil and hurt our economy. They use their financial resources to convince Congress to include provisions within legislation that will help enrich them, while hurting many other sectors of the economy or country. These types come in all shapes and sizes, and they generally have no awareness that they should do anything but help only themselves.

My point here is not to expound upon the negative side of mankind's nature, or to say that the enemy is everywhere. After living some life and traveling across the globe, it's my opinion that the vast majority of mankind is basically good at its core. The problem with our media- and Internet-driven culture is that dangerous, alarming and outrageous acts grab our attention, which means more viewers, more clicks and more sales for TV shows, websites and newspapers. Since that's what brings in the money, that's what they show the most, and we get a greatly distorted view of how dangerous our world is.

But we can't ignore the fact that there are those who would like us to fall from power. And so I ask you these questions:

Does our massive debt strengthen or weaken us?

Does it strengthen or weaken us to have huge interest payments that take up a portion of the money we're able to spend as a country?

Would you not rejoice if your enemy got overburdened with such a large amount of debt that it seemed unlikely they could ever repay it?

Wouldn't you love to have your enemy owe you a great deal of money?

How can we negotiate truly strong trade agreements, or push on human rights issues with a country such as China, when we owe them over a *trillion* dollars?

What would I do if I wanted to hurt the U.S. but couldn't take them on with direct military action? I'd quietly encourage them to overspend and get tied down with massive debt, spreading false information that it's smart and okay to have huge debt and to overspend each year. I'd find ways to keep the political parties in the U.S. battling each other, so that the country's board of directors remained divided and preoccupied with fighting each other instead of working together as a unified group to ensure that the U.S. government remained strong and free.

I consider our debt and our government's continual overspending a national security issue that needs to be addressed *now*, while we still have the power and means to get our financial house in order.

The good news for us—and the bad news for our adversaries—is that *we* are in charge of our country and there's still time for us to fix it.

"It is incumbent on every gencration to pay its own debts as it goes. A principle which, if acted on, would save one half the wars of the world."

—Thomas Jefferson in a letter written to French philosopher Antoine Louis Claude Destutt de Tracy on December 26, 1820

CHAPTER 17

Fragile Future

The New York Times
July 4, 2036

OBITUARIES

The United States of America

The United States of America, affectionately known as the USA, age 259, passed away on July 2, 2036, after defaulting on debt owed to some 120 world governments, its citizens eligible to receive Social Security and innumerable private investors, as well as other creditors. During bankruptcy talks with its top dozen debt holders and the World Bank, the former world power agreed to a dissolution of all government operations based on the once-mighty nation's original Constitution, ratified in 1789.

In a moving ceremony telecast around the globe, now-former U.S. president Laura Whitfield lowered the former republic's national flag, colloquially called the "Stars and Stripes," for the last time. The ceremony concluded with a worldwide online auction for the historic flag, with the winning bid contributing 2.4 million euros toward paying off the former country's debt of 30 trillion euro.

The country's Constitution, once called the "grand experiment" because of its novel approach, empowered the citizens to oversee their country by electing their government's leaders, an idea that has yet to find lasting success throughout history. But try it did, against all odds, and for a time the country was called a "superpower," commanding a military that had no equal on earth. For many decades, it led the world in scientific accomplishments that included being the first country to place a human on the moon. It also led the development of the computer age and the Internet, originally known as the "World Wide Web."

The unfortunate ailment that befell the country has been labeled by leading economic scholars simply as "Massive Debt Syndrome." Although all economically savvy world governments recognize that some debt is acceptable from time to time, the elected leaders of the United States seemed unable to contain its propensity for spending more than the country brought in from taxes and other revenue sources. Last year's Nobel Prize winner in economics, Professor Simone Wu, stated recently that had the country made a drastic change in key spending and political policies a decade or more ago, it would most likely still be alive and healthy today. And though many of its citizens tried to raise the alarm to get their government to change, not enough action was taken in time and the World Bank finally had to step in to oversee its dissolution.

With the former country dissolved, its creditors are now the primary stockholders of the newly formed corporation that oversees all activities of what were formerly the fifty states. The new organization has been named America, Inc., and those living within the boundaries of its land holdings, all the former states of the United Sates of America, can download their new laws and tax information at AmericaInc.us. The new CEO of America, Inc. will answer to a twenty-member board of directors elected by the organization's stockholders, the largest being the sovereign nation of China.

As is often mentioned when a friend dies prematurely, had more action been taken sooner to control the country's ballooning debt, we would not be mourning its passing, but instead celebrating its 260th birthday today.

The United States of America is survived by 270 million men, women and children. Should friends of the former republic so desire, donations to help pay off its obligations can be made online at the web address shown above.

What we're doing throughout this book is confronting a situation that exists in our country—our massive and ever-growing national debt—that no one else is doing anything about. We could liken it to a fire burning in the basement that is slowly eating away at the foundation and working its way up to the floors above. It certainly isn't pleasant to think about the fire, or do something about it, but ignoring it doesn't make it any less real or dangerous. And unless we at least prevent it from continuing to grow, we're going to have a much greater problem to deal with before long.

So since we're being so bold and looking at things that we'd rather not, let's consider this for a moment: What happens if we just continue to ignore the problem and do nothing about it? It doesn't seem like the debt has really hurt us up to this point, so why worry about it?

Earlier I wrote that interest rates will inevitably go up, and explored what that will mean for our American way of life, our ability to protect our country and other negative impacts. Okay, but let's play this out further, since so many (including our elected officials) are ignoring the problem. What's the big deal about having a lot of debt? Exactly who is going to try and collect from us if we fail to pay?

I think this is exactly what some people in our country and government probably think—who's going to do anything about it? Who's more powerful than we are? Who has the military might to foreclose on us? Though there are a million arguments against this type of strategy, it has an element of truth to it. The mafia, cartels and street thugs operate off this kind of logic quite successfully.

The only problem with this type of strategy is that if we just decide not to pay on our debts, then people, companies and governments around the world would most likely stop lending us money. If that were to occur, we'd have trouble covering our national expenditures, confidence in the American economy would plummet, people would stop spending and paying what they owe (home loans, car loans, credit card debt, etc.), companies wouldn't have enough revenue to pay workers, workers would stop working and so on, until our country came to a halt. At that point, there would likely be riots, looting and pandemonium.

Our problem is not someone coming after us militarily to collect on what we owe them. Our problem is keeping our economic system going and not violating the trust of those who invest in our government.

I have to confess at this point that for far too many years I've sat and wondered about this, without doing anything about it. The size and seemingly unsolvable nature of the problem immobilized me. I wondered if anyone in our government—or anywhere in the world— had any real solutions for it. With all the debt that we and most nations around the world have, could there possibly be a plan in which all the nations of the world would get together and agree to forgive each other's debt, and everyone would start over at a zero balance? Wouldn't that be great?

I think this idea comes from playing Monopoly or the Game of Life too many times over the years. At the end of the game, no matter how miserably you did, you could always start over.

So, can we just start the Game of Acquiring Debt over? If we did this, what would happen to Social Security and Medicare and the other large funds that we've all paid into over the years through deductions from our paychecks? These funds—which our government owes money to— are there to help pay for our retirement and health needs when we get older. If our government doesn't pay back what it owes to these funds, what happens to us when we get older? What about the two trillion dollars of debt that's owed to various mutual funds, local governments, insurance companies, retirement funds, banks and other investors? If we just forget about the debt to these groups, retirement funds would be severely damaged, the stock market would crash, insurance companies may have a hard time honoring legitimate insurance claims, local governments may need to cut back on services . . . and on and on.

The truth is, we took on the debt and there's no easy solution to get rid of it besides paying it off—which is probably too much to ask at this point. So let's go for at least maintaining the debt where it is, and *not* taking on any more!

If you're still holding onto the belief that the mighty U.S. could never fall—let's review a little world history.

The great ancient Egyptian civilization lasted around 3,000 years.[1] The civilization of ancient Greece is estimated to have lasted approximately 1,500 years.[2] Then came the Roman Empire, which existed for about 1,000 years.[3] And the English Empire—which ruled India and parts of Africa and developed Canada, Australia and our thirteen original colonies—effectively ended just after World War II, lasting approximately 500 years.[4]

And the United States? How do we stand up to these great civilizations? We're a powerful country, currently the most powerful in the world. Each of the civilizations previously mentioned was also the most powerful in the world during its time. But where are they now?

Despite their power, size, wealth and competence, none of them exist today. At some point, they crumbled and were overtaken by the next great empire.

Our country is currently less than 250 years old. And so it would seem—compared to the other great civilizations before us, many of which lasted over a thousand years—that we have a long way to go before our time is up.

But there's a problem with that point of view. You see, at our present youthful age, we're nearly the *oldest* country in the world. Out of approximately 195 countries around the world, there are only two that have had the same form of government longer than we have: England is one, and a tiny country in Europe named San Marino is the other.[5]

---

[1] The Ancient Egypt Site, "History of Ancient Egypt."

[2] Encyclopedia Britannica, "Ancient Greek Civilization."

[3] Ibid., "Ancient Rome."

[4] Ibid., "British Empire."

[5] Wikipedia, "List of Sovereign States by Date of Formation."

Does this strike you the same way it strikes me? We're one of the *oldest*, and we're not even 250 years old. We've been operating under the same form of government longer than the current governments of Russia, France, Spain, China, Germany, India and almost every other nation in the world.

As we all know, things move much faster than they used to. Information can travel around the globe in seconds. Economic upheaval can happen very quickly, as we all experienced in 2008. Governments can change rapidly, as we saw during the Arab Spring in 2010. It doesn't give me a lot of confidence that we're one of the oldest countries in the world and we haven't yet reached our 250th birthday.

The point of all this? *Civilizations are frail, and they don't last forever.*

If we had no debt and rarely spent more than we brought in, I might feel a little better about the likelihood that our civilization could last much longer. But with $18 trillion in debt—a number that is *growing* every year—it doesn't give me a lot of confidence. How about you?

Whenever I start thinking that something is really permanent, that it will last forever, I'm forced to look at the variety of seemingly immovable conditions, countries and/or governments that eventually collapsed and are no longer with us. In truth, *few* things are *truly* immovable or indestructible.

Why review all this? So that we understand exactly where we sit at this point in time with our government, so we can be smart about moving forward with a fix. If we're unaware of any problems, we may not even know there is anything to fix. And by missing the real look of things, and then doing nothing, one day we could easily find ourselves surprised when the economy crashes and it's *unfixable.*

Here are some historical examples of things that seemed impossible, but eventually became reality. When reviewing these points, understand that this swings both ways—it seems impossible that our government could ever fail when in fact it certainly *could*, and it also seems impossible that we could do anything to *fix* it when the truth is that we *can.*

FORMATION OF THE UNITED STATES OF AMERICA: Great Britain had ruled the colonies for some 170 years and was the most powerful country in the world at that time. The idea of our little undeveloped country—one without a regular army and no navy—declaring its independence from Great Britain and beating the British military seemed ridiculous, almost suicidal. But, as we know, we did defeat them. The seemingly impossible did happen.

SLAVERY: This was an institution that was in place in many parts of the world for thousands of years, and in the U.S. for hundreds (it still quietly exists in some parts of the world today). Despite its long-established history and resistance to its abolishment, slavery ended in the U.S. in 1865 with the passage of a new amendment to our Constitution (the Thirteenth Amendment) and a very bloody civil war.

BLACK CITIZENS' RIGHT TO VOTE: At the time of our country's formation, primarily only white male property owners were allowed to vote. But only five years after the slaves were freed, black men were granted this right, something that had been entirely unimaginable only a short time beforehand.

WOMEN'S RIGHT TO VOTE: For over a hundred years, women in the U.S. were mostly barred from voting. But in 1920, they finally won this right.

THE FALL OF THE IRON CURTAIN: At one time, there was a wall separating East and West Berlin, which also separated democracy from communism. It was built in 1961 and seemed incredibly permanent. But in 1989, with the fall of communism in East Germany, the wall literally came down and the Iron Curtain was no more.

THE END OF THE USSR: Our Cold War enemy for over forty years and the second most powerful country in the world at the time, the USSR collapsed in 1991. With this, the seemingly impossible became possible (partially because it had so much debt).

A BLACK PERSON ELECTED AS A U.S. PRESIDENT: Only forty years after our country was deeply divided on race issues and Martin Luther King Jr. was assassinated, Barack Obama was elected president of the most powerful country in the world—a historic day that few thought would ever occur. (Regardless of your views on President Obama, I think few would disagree that electing a black president was historic.)

If these substantial changes aren't enough for us to recognize how things *can* and *do* change (even when we think they never will), here are a few more: man's only been flying for a little over a hundred years, and we've only had electricity for a bit more than that; no one thought we'd launch a person into space, let alone ever land on the moon; and not long ago, we had eight-track tapes instead of CDs and iTunes.

Our world has changed dramatically in the last hundred years. Old, powerful institutions and countries are no longer the same—some have disappeared entirely. Is it too much to think that if *we* don't change our course of action, we might perish as well?

Regardless of whether we want it to or not, nothing lasts forever. Change is the norm, and is always happening.

But let's look at the positive side of this: our situation can also change for the *good* if we act appropriately and quickly. And thankfully, because of our very unique and powerful Constitution, it's in our power to do just that.

———————

"A house divided against itself cannot stand."

—Abraham Lincoln in a speech given to voters on
June 16, 1858, during his campaign for the U.S. Senate

———————

CHAPTER 18

No News Doesn't Mean Good News

THERE'S ONE MORE PIECE OF THIS PUZZLE THAT we need to talk about regarding our debt. As we discussed earlier, we like drama. We like watching and participating in competition and the game of one side trying to win by advancing against and then dominating the other. We see this every day in politics, between the two main political parties and the various elected officials arguing over an array of political issues such as health care, the environment, immigration and many others. All of this collision and competition makes for great content in the media and across the Internet.

But what happens to those issues that no one disagrees on? If there isn't a disagreement or conflict, if there isn't anything to fight about, compete over or debate? Lack of conflict and disagreement and competition doesn't make for very interesting reading or viewing, does it? No one clicks on the video with the title "No Conflict Between Husband and Wife—Watch Now." But a title that indicates great conflict in the article or video gets views and clicks. This is how the media game works—write about or show conflict and people will read or watch it, and that usually translates into revenue. But there isn't any financial incentive to write about things that we all agree on, which means that they're *rarely written about.*

This is exactly the case with our national debt situation, because it's one issue we can almost all agree on—that it isn't good. Pretty hard to find anyone who will argue that we need *more* debt and need to overspend *more* year after year. Because of this, it doesn't show up in the media, it isn't a regular point of conversation and it isn't a "hot issue."

Another reason we don't see our debt problem in the press is that it's so overwhelming, and it feels like there's nothing we can do about it. It's depressing, everyone agrees it's bad and no one really knows what to do about it. So it doesn't get talked about.

But does that mean it isn't important to the future welfare of our country? Hardly. Just because it isn't on the front page and people aren't rioting in the streets over it doesn't mean it isn't extremely important to us and everyone who comes after us. True, it doesn't fit into the game of being full of good drama and conflict. But that doesn't mean it isn't important. The truth is, it's absolutely vital that we do something about it.

"I consider the fortunes of our republic as depending, in an eminent degree, on the extinguishment of the public debt, before we engage in any war, because, that done, we shall have revenue enough to improve our country in peace, and defend it in war, without recurring either to new taxes or loans. . . . The discharge of the debt therefore is vital to the destinies of our government."

—Thomas Jefferson in a letter written to the U.S. Secretary of the Treasury on October 11, 1809, shortly after his second term as president

CHAPTER 19

Not My Problem

I HAVE A FRIEND WHO USED TO SAY THIS frequently about various things he encountered in life: "Not my problem."

At first I was a bit taken aback by this. I thought it was an irresponsible attitude. Although I eventually learned what my friend meant by this and what he was (correctly) directing it at, and although there *are* situations in which this approach is valid (which I'll get into in a minute), there are far too many people who see what's happening in their country and think, "Not my problem." It's so easy for us to blame all our country's problems on our elected officials or government workers. Too many people blame everything on the other party—the one they don't belong to.

If you gain nothing else from this book, I hope you will be able to see how *anything* going wrong with your country is your problem. And that you're not alone—that it's a problem we are *all* ultimately responsible for. It just isn't smart to put the blame on others, because it doesn't fix anything. Even if it *is* someone else's fault, even if they really are to blame, we still need to ensure that the problem gets fixed because, as we discussed earlier, if the ship goes down, we all go down with it. It's in our best interest—all of us—to make sure our country is secure, financially sound and healthy.

I know, that's a lot of responsibility to deal with. The good news is that there *is* an area that you can say isn't your problem. We as members of the board don't have to know how to fix our country's problems, just as the board of directors of Apple or Google doesn't have to know how to run those companies or how to fix their problems. That's *management's* job. We're on the board of directors. Our job is to make sure management does *their* job. Period. End of story. That's our job! We must ensure that management does their job, or put new management in place who will!

And what's management's job? As we discussed earlier in the book, their job is to fulfill the purposes for our government as laid out in our Constitution. Here they are again:

1. To form a more perfect union

2. To establish justice

3. To ensure domestic tranquility

4. To provide for the common defense

5. To promote the general welfare

6. To secure the blessings of liberty for ourselves and posterity

This is what the government that we've sanctioned and authorized to exist is supposed to be doing for us. It's starting to look a little less complicated, isn't it?

Those we elect to work for us need to be fulfilling these purposes for our government. And let me just say, in case there's any misunderstanding—if they aren't doing this, they either need to *start* doing it or they need to be *replaced*.

Am I being too harsh? Is this too intense or too mean? That's for you to decide. But keep in mind that *they* work for *you*. They're managing your government and your tax dollars and they're either helping or hurting your country—the country that will be inherited by your children, your friends, their children and everyone else who comes after you. And by the way, let's not forget that you're paying their salary and benefits. You pay for their office space, the pencils they use and the government planes they fly in. You pay the salaries of their staff and bodyguards. No matter how you look at it, they work for you, and ultimately they *answer to you*. You oversee them . . . or at least you have the power to. Whether or not you use that power is *up to you*.

The point here is that if there's something going wrong with our country, it *is* your problem, but how to fix it *isn't*. You, as a member of our country's board of directors, select and hire the management team you want in place to effectively run your country. It's that team's responsibility to run our government in a way that fulfills the purposes laid out for them. They need to do *their* job, and we need to do *ours*.

"Let us not despair but act. Let us not seek the Republican answer or the Democratic answer but the right answer. Let us not seek to fix the blame for the past—let us accept our own responsibility for the future."

—Senator John F. Kennedy in a speech given at
Loyola College on February 18, 1958

CHAPTER 20

We the People

IN 1776, THE INHABITANTS OF THE THIRTEEN British colonies on the eastern coast of our country declared their independence from Great Britain, which tried to use military action to prevent the colonies from splitting.

Newly independent from British rule, the inhabitants of the colonies formed a governing body of their own called the Continental Congress and each colony—now independent states—elected representatives to make up the new Congress. That Congress, in turn, needed a set of rules by which the thirteen states could operate together in order to run their new country and fend off the British military invasion.

The rules they developed were written out in a document, our country's first constitution, called the Articles of Confederation and Perpetual Union, which held the new country together well enough to get through the war that lasted until 1783.

After the war was over, as the country recovered and started organizing and establishing itself and getting recognized by foreign governments, it became very apparent that the Articles of Confederation and Perpetual Union, though useful during the extreme emergency of the war, was grossly ineffective for the new country to grow and thrive.

So in 1786, as twelve delegates representing five different states were meeting in Annapolis, Maryland, to work out various commercial trade disputes, they concluded that the only way to truly resolve the disputes was to make changes to the Articles of Confederation and Perpetual Union. So they wrote to the states and Congress requesting a national meeting in Philadelphia (the largest city in the nation at that point) to fix the country's constitution. Because of all the problems in the country, people wholeheartedly agreed with the idea, and approximately eight months later representatives from the various states began arriving in Philadelphia. Though they were only authorized to propose *changes* to the Articles of Confederation, the fifty-five men who showed up in Philadelphia decided that what was needed was an entirely *new* constitution.

Those representatives of the first citizens of the United States put together a blueprint for a new government for our country. That blueprint was voted on and approved by the citizens of the thirteen states of our country. And that document—our Constitution—legally authorized the formation of a government to work on their behalf in a very specific and limited way to achieve the six purposes assigned to it.

Each point and principle in the document was debated. Those at the meeting were some of the brightest minds in the country, and many had extensively researched and experienced the best and worst of government. Many of them were veterans of the Revolutionary War. They all worked over four hot, humid months in Philadelphia to put down in written form the guidelines for a government that would be subservient to the citizens it served—an extremely rare and bold idea at that time in history.

I'm sharing this simple backdrop to clearly illuminate to us all that our government was established *solely by and for the citizens of our country*. Yes, those first citizens in the late 1700s wrote the document and ratified it, but we as citizens *inherit that same power and responsibility* that they had in authorizing and overseeing their government. It was *their* government, it's now *our* government, and in the future, it will be *our children's* government.

Our Constitution is timeless. Its job is to forever be the supreme guide for our country to follow. It was written in such a way that it will *always* and *only* serve the citizens of our country, regardless of income, education, religion, race, sexual orientation, employment status or place of birth. It is almost as if by magic that, when a new citizen is born or an immigrant takes the official Oath of Allegiance, our Constitution immediately and automatically becomes subservient to them, and thereafter exclusively works on their behalf. A continual, peaceful transfer of power and servitude happens as citizens die and new ones emerge.

Only a short span of time has passed since our Constitution was first ratified and put into use. Yes, the document has been amended some, but mostly to grant more rights to the citizens who oversee it. The document's first three words—"we the people"—mean the same thing today as they did when they were written. Though our government is massive, powerful and dominant in the world, we *alone* allow its power and authority to exist and act.

But just as the early citizens of our country worked to birth it, we must *actively* work to keep it alive, healthy and on the right track. Don't we owe that to those early citizens, to ourselves and to our children and others who will inherit the reins of our country after we're gone?

I hope you can see that the United States of America is, without a doubt, very clearly and legally *our* country, and that the government running it does so *only* on our behalf and for our benefit.

"Let us not be afraid to help each other—let us never forget that government is ourselves and not an alien power over us. The ultimate rulers of our democracy are not a President and Senators and Congressmen and Government officials but the voters of this country."

—President Franklin D. Roosevelt in a speech given in Marietta, Ohio, on July 8, 1938

CHAPTER 21

Management Qualifications

HOPEFULLY AT THIS POINT YOU SEE THE POWER you have over your government, and that it works on your behalf. And as we discussed earlier, your position can be likened to that of a member of the board of directors of our country. From that position, your job is to ensure that the managers you select to oversee your government are doing a good job and fulfilling their purpose as laid out by our Constitution.

But how do we choose who should be part of that management team? Based on the frustration most people feel when it comes to their elected officials, and based on the fact that our government has overspent for seventy-two years out of the last eighty-four, I would say that how we've been doing it up to this point needs to change.

There's no doubt that our system is broken and needs some adjustment. But if we'd really done a good job of picking excellent representatives, wouldn't they have done their job and fixed the system themselves, on our behalf, and not saddled us with a debt that realistically can never be paid back? Wouldn't they have figured out a way on their own to repair the pitfalls in the system and come up with ways to avoid overspending in eighty-six percent of the years since 1931? True, those who've run our government haven't made *all* bad decisions in the last eighty-four years, but they *have* erred dangerously with our country's finances—to the point where, unless we step in and force them to properly do their jobs, our country could be significantly, and possibly irreparably, harmed.

Let's be clear about this. The government works on our behalf and we elect the managers who oversee it, and their job is to ensure that our government fulfills its purposes as spelled out in our Constitution. That's how simple it is. And there's no reason why the managers we put in place shouldn't do their jobs, and do them well! Do they have tough jobs? For sure. Is running a government a complex and difficult task? Yes, no doubt! But can it actually be done? Absolutely! So why isn't it being done? For a number of reasons we discussed earlier in this book, as well as one additional reason that we'll discuss in this chapter: we may not be picking qualified candidates to represent us in Washington.

Let's take a look at what one of our elected representatives in Congress or the White House has to manage on our behalf:

1. Overseeing our national security, including the long-term strategic development of our military technology, equipment, personnel and alliances.

2. Developing our national budget and spending our tax dollars wisely so as to improve our country for the long-term benefit of all.

3. Diligently and wisely working to increase our strength, power and position in the world in such a way that allows the countries of earth to live in the greatest degree of harmony and cooperation as possible; to keep our country at full strength, but in a way that also allows as many countries as possible to thrive and prosper to achieve freedom and happiness for their citizens as well.

4. Regulating and controlling the various industries and businesses

in our country in a way that allows them maximum survival and prosperity, while also reasonably protecting our country's resources, environment and citizens.

5. Ensuring that the very document that gives them the power to exist—our Constitution—is closely adhered to, both in what is clearly laid out in writing within that document and with regard to its overall general meaning and spirit.

6. Developing and passing new laws that comply with our Constitution and enhance our ability to live safely and prosperously and to pursue our happiness.

7. Protecting our rights and in general working in our best interest.

There are definitely more duties they need to fulfill, but the above list at least gives us an idea of the scope of what they should be doing, and the skill set they should have. Ideally, we'd like them to be doing their jobs well, wouldn't we? Well, doesn't it follow that those we send in to oversee our government should be *qualified* for their jobs? Isn't that exactly what every successful business and organization does when it fills open positions in its management team?

So why don't we do this with our government? Too often, we base the decision on personal preferences rather than hard qualifications. We watch a candidate on TV or meet them in person and are influenced by how well they speak, or how attractive they are. Yes, there's no doubt that good communication skills and personal grooming and dress are important qualities in a leader. But shouldn't we be voting for candidates with successful track records of balancing budgets and running organizations, regardless of their political party? Here's just a partial list of experience, skills and abilities that our representatives should ideally possess.

A highly successful track record:

1. Running a group or organization

2. Balancing budgets

3. Developing and executing fair and beneficial long-term strategic plans that have created increased benefits for an organization and the customers or public it served

4. Working with varied groups in a way that helped benefit all

5. Demonstrating that he or she has integrity and is morally upright, unbigoted, fair, honest and tolerant

6. Handling power with little self-interest and with equity toward others

7. Demonstrating an abiding care, respect and love for our country and its well-being, as well as those citizens it belongs to

8. Correctly making difficult decisions that may be unpopular but necessary for the long-term benefit of an organization or community

The list could go on and on—and it *should*.

In the end, shouldn't it be a privilege and honor to be selected to represent us and manage our government? One that doesn't just suggest popularity, but instead signifies incredible competence, leadership, integrity and proven success? Shouldn't a position on the management team running our government be not only a supreme honor, but also the ultimate validation of that person's skills and abilities?

One of the key problems we face when electing top-tier candidates to our management team is that most people have no interest in running for office. Some of our best and brightest—those running successful businesses and organizations—aren't interested in going through the election gauntlet, where negative personal attacks are the norm. As a result, our options are unfortunately not always the best people for the job. But we're forced to choose between them, and sometimes none of the choices on the election ballot are really very good.

When a company is looking to hire someone, they aren't forced to choose between a few candidates if they aren't happy with any of them. They can leave the position open and keep looking for the right person. Unfortunately, we don't have that option when choosing who's going to represent us on our government's management team.

But wouldn't it shake things up if we did have that option? What if there was a "none of the above" option on every ballot? If we didn't like any of the candidates, we could just choose "none of the above." Yes, it would certainly disrupt the steady flow of government, but maybe that's exactly what it needs. If "none of the above" got the majority of votes, what if another election could be scheduled in thirty days? And we kept holding elections until someone received the majority of votes? That would certainly change how the political game is played.

Yes, there are obstacles standing in the way of us being able to choose the best people to represent us. But the first step is understanding what qualifications we require of our management team. With that clearly understood, we can then begin attracting those types of individuals by electing them when they step forward. We also need to recognize these types of people within our communities and personally urge them to become candidates. And if they're attacked when they do step forward, we need to defend, help and back them up. We need good, ethical, highly successful people working on our behalf, but we won't get them unless we fully support them.

There are other things we could do to help attract better candidates, but I think that might be the subject of another book. My goal for this book is not to solve that particular problem. But I think it's important and valid for us all—as members of our country's board of directors—to understand what type of individuals we should be selecting. With this better understanding, let's send truly good, successful people to manage our government in D.C.

Just a final note on this point. During my research on pressing the reset button, I read a great deal about the various individuals who were instrumental in the very early stages of our country, as well as those who were members of the group that wrote our Constitution. Many of these individuals were our first elected representatives, serving in our first Congress. Many went on to serve in prominent roles within our government, including the position of president. What struck me about many of these individuals was how incredibly intelligent, well-read and successful they were.

One example is John Adams, who could read both Latin and Greek. He was extremely well-read and searched out new books throughout his life. When he was assigned by Congress to represent the new U.S. in France, he picked up much of the French language so he could perform his duties to the best of his ability. Mr. Adams personally wrote the Massachusetts Constitution, which is still in use today. He was a member of Congress before becoming our country's first vice president and then its second president. By the end of his life, it's estimated that his personal library contained some 3,200 books.

Another example is Thomas Jefferson, who spoke Latin, Greek, French and Italian and had a partial understanding of various Native American languages. He was an inventor, writer, musician, lawyer, archeologist, farmer, architect, builder, poet and much more. He designed and founded the University of Virginia. He wrote much of the Declaration of Independence. He served in U.S. public office as the governor of Virginia, the minister to France, the first secretary of state, the second vice president and the third president. During his presidency, he purchased a huge section of land from France in the middle of our country called the Louisiana Purchase, and sent Lewis and Clark on an expedition to find a land route to the Pacific Ocean, among other purposes.

And then there was Alexander Hamilton, a great writer and speaker who was one of the authors of *The Federalist Papers*, a series of articles written in favor of our Constitution's ratification.

Another was James Madison, who is credited with developing the overall basic blueprint for our Constitution.

The list goes on and on. The people who helped create our country and fight off the most powerful military force in the world at that time—Great Britain—were a rare and special group, and many of them were incredibly well-educated, talented and successful, not to mention brave and dedicated to our country.

Why shouldn't the managers we elect today be of the same caliber as those who formed and led our country in the beginning? The complexities of governing certainly haven't lessened over time. We have an immense need for bright ideas and smart solutions to many of the problems facing our country today. We need the bright, smart and able as part of the management team overseeing our government. Let's find and encourage them to run, and when they do, let's help and protect them.

———————

"I hope I shall always possess firmness and virtue enough to maintain (what I consider the most enviable of all titles) the character of an honest man, as well as prove (what I desire to be considered in reality) that I am."

—George Washington in a letter written to Alexander Hamilton on August 28, 1788

———————

CHAPTER 22

Our Power

NOW THAT YOU'VE WALKED THE PATH OF discovery to find our country's reset button just as I did, let's get down to it. How do we press the reset button when our government is off-track and not performing as it should?

It's very simple: we use the power granted to us in the Constitution to act as our country's board of directors.

We use the one and only absolute power we have, which is *the power of the vote*.

Anything else we do to voice our opinion regarding our government is non-binding and can be *ignored* by the government. We can march in protest, write letters to our representatives, make huge donations to one party or another, sign petitions and many, many other things. Though these actions can be useful in bringing about change, our government has no obligation to change anything because of it. In the end, as is clearly laid out in our Constitution, the true power to change and influence our government resides *within each of us and our right to vote*.

Of our government, the Declaration of Independence states: "It is the Right of the People to alter or to abolish it, and to institute new Government, laying its foundation on such principles and organizing its powers in such form, as to them shall seem most likely to effect their Safety and Happiness."[1]

---

[1] Like the Constitution, the Declaration of Independence was written at a time when it was common practice to capitalize important nouns in the middle of sentences.

Those who wrote our Constitution were *very* concerned about creating a government that would grow out of control and fail to work in the best interest of the people. They'd had their own trouble with King George, and found the government designed by the Articles of Confederation and Perpetual Union to be inadequate. So as they re-designed our government, they built in a system—a reset button—that would allow the citizens of the country to peacefully overthrow the government if they felt it warranted, without spilling any blood. It's actually a brilliant safeguard, and one that has never been fully put to use, to my knowledge.

But it will only work if we all act together. If we do, the change in our government will be sweeping and substantial.

This is what each of us needs to do:

1. Register to vote.

2. On Election Day, get yourself to the place where you're supposed to vote (or fill out and mail in your absentee ballot).

3. Enter the voting booth.

4. Based on the government's performance fulfilling its six purposes for existence as laid out in the Constitution, determine whether our government is doing well or not.

5. If you think the government is doing poorly, vote for every person running who is *new* and isn't currently part of the government. If you think the government is doing well, vote as you would normally for the candidate you like best and the various issues you feel strongly about.

6. Turn in your ballot.

7. Feel good that you voted in a way that will change our country.

That's it. That's how simple it is. Now, there might be situations where this method doesn't work. For example, if the person currently in office isn't running again, *all* the candidates will be new. The best way to approach this situation is to just pick whatever candidate you like because, in the end, you have no choice but to vote for someone new.

What if your favorite congressperson is a really good person who tries hard, and you like him or her? Are you supposed to vote him or her out if the country is doing poorly? Without question, that is your choice, and a decision you'll need to make before you vote. But I encourage you to strongly consider it. He or she is part of the current management team, and if they have been driving us further into debt—for whatever reason—they should be removed to allow others a shot at making things go the right way.

Would you keep a management team in a business you owned if they performed poorly? Would you be okay if this management team continued putting you in debt and seemed to not pay close attention to what you, and the others they served, really needed?

It isn't okay for them to do this. It's wrong, and it's damaging to leave a group in place that is responsible for running our government in a way that hurts our country and our future.

If enough voters followed this system of voting, our government would dramatically change. In just six years—just three elections—we could have an entire new House of Representatives, Senate and president. All of them, *new*. And do you think those elected into office by voters using this method would know that the people (the board of directors) were now paying attention and meant business? Most certainly. They would understand that unless they got the government working for the *people* first, they would be out in the very next election. If we all voted this way in every election, we would turn our government over until management figured out a way to truly fulfill its purpose.

Those board members who think Congress is doing a good or excellent job

everyone else

Source: Data from Rasmussen Reports (2015).

If this idea just seems too simple to really work, I understand. It is very simple. But it *will* work, if we all vote in this very sensible and, yes, simple way. Don't brush it off because it's simple. Some of the best and most powerful ideas are very simple.

If the idea causes you concern or makes you feel a little uneasy, I understand that as well. This is a completely different look at elections. We aren't talking about who belongs to which party. We aren't talking about candidates' personalities or what they wear or how they look. We're only considering their performance in their jobs, and if they've been doing it well. If they're in office and they haven't been doing their jobs, if the country is going broke and they're affecting the long-term stability of the U.S. by repeatedly allowing the government to overspend, they need to be elected out so a new batch of citizens can have a shot at running things. Isn't that how it should be? Shouldn't they be removed if they're part of the group that's hurting our country? So why not vote with that in mind?

Ultimately, *you* are a member of the board of directors, and *only you* can decide how you will vote. I encourage you to think this idea through, look at it for yourself and use your power of the vote in a way that you think is best for both the short- and long-term health of our country.

In the end, the process should be quick and easy. But without you, nothing will happen. If enough of us vote in this way, our country will, without question, come back under our control. With that done, we can start moving forward with fixing the other important issues facing our country that affect us all.

"The people of these United States are the rightful masters of both Congresses and courts, not to overthrow the Constitution, but to overthrow the men who pervert the Constitution."

—Abraham Lincoln in a speech delivered in Cincinnati, Ohio, on September 17, 1859, less than a year before he was nominated for president

CHAPTER 23

Together

O UR COUNTRY HAS BEEN MOVING DOWN THE same political path since shortly after our Constitution was ratified. When our country was formed, our biggest problem was winning freedom from Great Britain. We were unified as a nation against a much superior foe, and that contest had our full attention. All of us were on one team, and Great Britain and those who remained loyal to her were on the other side. Lives were literally at stake. Those who signed the Declaration of Independence would have surely hung for treason if the colonies lost the war, and the colonial citizens would have had the British army occupying and ruling over them for years. A great deal of freedom was at stake.

As I mentioned earlier, when George Washington was elected as our first president, there were no political parties, and they aren't mentioned in the Constitution. They weren't designed by our country's founders to be part of our government. There wasn't a consultant who flew in from Europe and counseled our leaders to start the various parties. They happened naturally, and shortly after our Constitution was ratified, they began to take shape. They formed out of the need for people with similar interests to have enough power and leverage to get their voices heard.

Political parties have dominated our politics and how we elect our representatives for over 200 years. They were specifically designed to coordinate the power you and I have as members of our country's board of directors. Have they been beneficial to our country and to all of us?

That's for you to decide. But this is what I know: They have divided us. They've become a way for us to create drama and competition. They've given us a way to argue about and fight for what we want against those who don't want the same things. And in some respects, I'm not so sure that either side always cares very deeply about the issues themselves; sometimes it seems like it's just about winning the argument.

During our war to win our independence, we were generally unified. After we won, we were mainly on the same side for a period of time, and then we split into teams and have been fighting amongst ourselves ever since. Because of this, we've lost sight of our true mission as members of the board—to always strive for what's in our best long-term interest as a country. We've lost sight of the fact that *we* oversee our government, not the other way around. We've lost sight of the fact that our government was formed by *us*, that its only power comes from *us* and that it's simply there to manage our country for *us*.

We've fought amongst ourselves to the point that we're over $18 trillion in debt—an embarrassingly and disgracefully astronomical amount. We've distracted ourselves with our desire to play a game against each other, to engage in competition and fight for whatever it is we think is so important.

Don't get me wrong—many of the things we've fought for over the centuries have been important. The fight to give black citizens their freedom and the right to vote, winning the right for women to vote, the civil rights movement and many, many other issues that we've all fought for have been very significant. But we're at a point in history where our infighting and dividedness have led to true potential financial calamity.

Yes, we've allowed ourselves to become distracted. So be it. But that doesn't mean we can't learn from our mistakes and correct them going forward. Political parties are completely natural and will never go away. But we need to understand what they were designed to do, and how they can cause harm by dividing us, if we allow it. We need to use them when it's best for the country, and stand above and outside them when we need to act together for the greater good of our country.

We need to make a course correction—and doing so is almost too easy. We simply need to use our power together, at the same time and in the same direction. And it needs to be done by all of us, not just half of us.

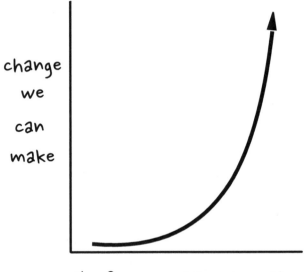

change
we
can
make

# of us working together

The fifty-five people who wrote our Constitution were very different from each other in many ways. Some were lawyers; others were farmers. Some were scientists; others were real estate developers. Some were ministers; others worked in education. Some were wealthy; others were not. And of course, since they were representatives of the various states, they came from different parts of the country and had different customs and accents. They were very different people who found a way to work together for the greater good of the citizens of the brand-new United States.

In they end, they were unanimous in ratifying the Constitution. Every state in the union held a vote to ratify it, and although only nine states needed to approve for it to go into effect, every state voted in favor of it. Were there arguments for and against ratification? Absolutely. But in the end, it was ratified by every state.

It's important to realize that we *can* work together when our country needs us to. We actually aren't as different from each other as the various parties and the media would have us believe. In the end, we're all primarily here in the United States for the same reason we broke away from Great Britain in 1776, and for the same reason millions of people have immigrated to our country over the centuries (and still do today)—for *freedom*. Deep down, at the core of us all, is the desire for freedom. And in our country, even though we aren't perfect, we have many valuable and important freedoms, as delineated in the Constitution.

Our Constitution was written over a period of four months in sweltering Philadelphia summer heat. No one—including those who wrote it—has claimed that it's perfect. And the brilliance of it is that we can adjust it if we feel it's necessary. It is a constant work in progress, and it's gotten us successfully to this point. Now we just need to use the powers it grants us to reset our country and make a course correction.

It's *our* country. Whether we like it or not, it's our job to oversee it. And when you take away all the clutter, noise, confusion, dissent, party politics and media opinion, our job is actually incredible easy and the power we wield is supreme. We just need to take action and wield it—and wield it wisely.

"This is a time for courage and a time for challenge. Neither conformity nor complacency will do. . . . So let us not be petty when our cause is so great. Let us not quarrel amongst ourselves when our Nation's future is at stake. Let us stand together with renewed confidence in our cause—united in our heritage of the past and our hopes for the future—and determined that this land we love shall lead all mankind into new frontiers of peace and abundance."

—President John F. Kennedy in a speech he had written and was scheduled to deliver in Dallas on the evening of November 22, 1963, the day he was assassinated

CHAPTER 24

After Reset

THERE'S NO DOUBT THAT AFTER WE PRESS THE reset button and replace our government's management team, there's going to be some confusion. It might even look a little chaotic. This is to be expected whenever there's a change to how things have always been done and old, established systems are discarded.

Have you ever had a closet that you just ached to clean out and rearrange? Remember what happened when you pulled everything out? It probably looked a bit confused, with various items scattered around and out of their normal positions. But when you threw out everything that was unneeded and put things back in a more orderly fashion, it most likely not only looked better, but you probably actually *felt* better about it.

It's natural that when going from one state or condition to another, there's going to be some confusion in-between. But just because there's confusion doesn't mean the end result is going to be bad, or that you've made things worse. What it signifies is that you're headed in the right direction, and the right thing to do is continue!

People don't necessarily like change. Habits are formed for a very good reason—they make the daily operations of life easier, since they're more automatic and take less of our attention. If you're feeling some resistance to the idea of pressing our country's reset button, you may simply be running up against your own natural desire to have things run the way they always have. The trick is recognizing that it's just resistance to change, and not necessarily resistance to something bad or destructive.

Remember that change, and even destruction, isn't necessarily bad if the change destroys old habits and systems that have been causing *more* destruction. If there's a fire in the basement of your home, causing change by putting it out is obviously the wise choice, even if your basement gets flooded with water in the process. If there's a leak in the hull of a ship, even if it's been there for a long time and is somehow seen as "beneficial" to the survival of all aboard, if it threatens the survival of the ship, change will need to be made to that leak in the form of a repair.

By pressing our country's reset button, we're going to cause change—much-needed change—and that will cause some disruption. This isn't necessarily bad, it's just disruption. Then, while we have everything pulled out of the closet and spread all over the room, we'll make some intelligent tweaks to the system, and then let it all fall back into place to operate in a way that's more conducive to a better future for our country.

As mentioned in Chapter 15, one of the changes we need to implement is adjusting how money flows to our elected representatives, and how it is used to influence elections. In my opinion, this is the number-one change we need to make to disrupt business as usual in Washington and obliterate management's long-established destructive governing habits—which got us into the dismal financial condition we're in today.

How can we make that change happen? We can send very clear messages to our management team that this is what we want done. The first message we send will be on Election Day, when we cast our votes to remove the old management team and give a new team a chance. Is it likely that we're going to be able to replace everyone in office? No, it's not. But we don't need to in order for our message to be understood.

There are approximately 225 million eligible voters in our country. That's 225 million board members eligible to cast a vote for the management team they want in place to oversee their government. But in past elections, a large percentage of them haven't used their right to vote, thus allowing others to make the decision of who should run their country for them. In the 2012 presidential election, forty-three percent of those who could have voted didn't, which is approximately 96 million board members. In the 2014 midterm elections, it's estimated that sixty-four percent of those who could have voted didn't, or about 144 million board members.[1] That's how many *didn't* use their power. (By the way, voter turnout for the 2014 election was the *lowest it's been in seventy years*.)

To me, these numbers are staggering. If just those board members who haven't been voting in past elections stepped forward in the next national election and voted as outlined in this book, our country would be changed. In many congressional races, a small percentage of votes separates the winner from the losers. Even if only a small percentage of those who didn't participate in the last election were to vote in the 2016 national elections, much of the existing management team would most likely be removed.

Fortunately, we live in a free country that also grants each of us the freedom to not only vote *how* we want, but also to vote *if* we want. This is a wonderful freedom that means those who haven't been voting can just as easily change their minds and decide to vote. And with their votes, they can substantially change our country.

As I wrote earlier in this chapter, the first message we'll send will be on Election Day, when members of the board will press the reset button and vote management out.

The next message will come from us directly via letters, emails, phone calls and any other form of direct communication that we can have with the various members of our management team. We will tell them not only that they need to quit overspending, but also that they need to systemically change how money flows to elected officials and political candidates, and how it's used to influence the outcome of elections.

---

[1] United States Election Project, "2014 November General Election Turnout Rates."

The bottom line: it's our management team's *job* to fix the system. Our job was putting them in office. The truth is that very intelligent, well-intentioned people and organizations have been trying to remove money from politics for a long time. Excellent ideas already exist; they just need to be implemented. Management needs to sort through the various plans, pick the best ones and make them law. And, if they think the Supreme Court will rule that the new laws violate our Constitution, then management needs to simply amend it.

I use the word "simply" here intentionally. All of this is simple if we want to make it happen, because the Constitution is *our* document—it is subservient to us. It's simply our blueprint for how our government is to structure itself and function. If we adjust it, we adjust our government. Those who drafted the Constitution knew that it would need adjusting as times changed, and so they built in a simple mechanism that only we can trigger, either through our management team in Washington or our elected officials in the various state legislatures.

So what happens if they don't listen to us and they don't fix the system, and things continue down the wrong path for our country? Then we press the reset button again in the next election, vote that management team out and put a new team in place. And we continue doing this until we're satisfied that the country is again moving in a healthy direction that will ensure our country's long-term strength, prosperity and survival.

Is pressing the reset button a perfect solution? No, it's not, but in truth those rarely, if ever, occur in life. Will pressing the reset button cause change, get the attention of our management team and have the greatest chance of truly altering the course of our country?

There's no doubt about it to me, but ultimately, *you're* going to have to make that decision for yourself. It's your freedom and right to use your power as a member of our country's board of directors as you choose. If you do decide to use your power as I've suggested here, a clear message will be transmitted, alerting our government and the world that *we the people* are in charge of the United States of America.

―――――――――――

"I do not conceive that we are more inspired—have more wisdom—or possess more virtue than those who will come after us. The power under the Constitution will always be with the people. It is entrusted for certain defined purposes and for a certain limited period to representatives of their own choosing; and whenever it is exercised contrary to their interests, or not according to their wishes, their servants can, and undoubtedly will be, recalled."

—George Washington to his nephew Bushrod Washington on November 9, 1787, two months after the Constitution was written

―――――――――――

CHAPTER 25

National Security

EARLIER IN THE BOOK I BROUGHT UP THE point that our country's debt is ultimately a national security issue. Our security is so fundamentally important to us that I think we need to look at this a bit closer.

While we've been fighting amongst ourselves, someone—an enemy to a greater or lesser degree—pretending to be acting in our best interest has convinced us and our management that having debt is good for our country. Put another way, while we were distracted and had our guard down, someone—or a group of someones—subtly slipped us some bad information that we mistook for truth. We used that information and the overspending began, usually explained away as being "for the greater good" of the country. There's no question that some emergency situations may require taking on debt to handle an immediate threat or national problem, but those should be few and far between if management is doing its job well. We certainly shouldn't have needed to overspend for seventy-two out of the last eighty-four years.

This false notion that "debt is okay" is so prevalent that even economic "experts" can be found repeating it on national news programs and in leading publications. Whether they're aware of it or not, by simply repeating the false information—which gives it credibility because they're thought of as experts—they are literally acting as enemy agents. And as our national debt has grown, we've all become accustomed to the idea that nothing can be done about it or about our government's constant overspending. As a nation, we've become numb to these problems. It's as if we've thrown up our hands in utter frustration and just accepted that we're powerless about it. And all the while, our enemies have been cheering.

In order for us to ensure that our country stays healthy and strong and is a great place to live, each of us as members of the board must remain vigilant for those droplets of truth coming at us in the waterfall of information we process each day. We need to watch for fundamental principles that work and improve our country. We need to act on recommended courses of action that lead to a stronger country for us all. We need government policy that increases the life span of our country, and we need to reject "facts" that appear to be true and that "everyone knows" are true, but are in fact *false*.

And what is our test to determine if something is true or false? First, we each usually know when something we hear is true or false—too often, we ignore our instincts. But another way of determining truth or falsehood is seeing whether that idea or principle works.

In the field of engineering, this test is easy: when you build a bridge based on false principles, it falls. It can be harder to tell whether something works when it comes to less scientific subjects, like government. But if you've ever taken on too much debt, you probably learned very quickly that the broad general statement of "debt is good" is absolutely untrue.

In order to stay strong and powerful as a nation in our rapidly advancing world, our government needs to be efficient, smart, properly focused and *expertly* managed. The management team we put in place to oversee our government for us needs to be extremely skilled, intelligent, moral and knowledgeable (and, ideally, experienced) in multiple areas, including finance, international relations, law, human rights and many more.

We as a nation need to think ahead and develop energy sources that will ensure our independence and strength. We should have a financial *surplus* stored away in safe depositories and invested brilliantly. We should have an extremely efficient, knowledgeable, skilled, rapid and modern military. We should have a nation that understands how to properly educate its youth without breaking them of their imagination and drive, while ensuring that they have the skills and knowledge to survive well in our modern world.

MUST

Congressional ^To-Do list

☑ <u>Stop overspending</u>

☑ Keep Country Safe

☑ Make Country More
   Energy-Independent

☑ Educate Youth BETTER

I could go on and on about this, as I'm sure you also could, but what we really need to understand is that all of these "shoulds" *are* possible, and that they *can* happen. *None* of them are beyond our grasp and ability as a nation. We are brilliant, innovative, industrious and creative. There's *no* reason that our government shouldn't perfectly reflect those same qualities. But as the overseers of our government, we must do *our* job of holding those we elect to the management team accountable, and not be afraid to make drastic changes to that team when necessary. We must recognize factors that make us weaker and less healthy as a country. We must constantly stay alert for falsehoods when they crop up, and loudly label them for what they are so that everyone can see the *truth*.

You and I must do our jobs of ensuring that our elected management team does its duty to keep our country secure, strong and healthy.

The good news is that our job isn't difficult or time-consuming, but it does require our involvement every two years.

"Let every nation know, whether it wishes us well or ill, that we shall pay any price, bear any burden, meet any hardship, support any friend, oppose any foe to assure the survival and the success of liberty."

—President John F. Kennedy in his inauguration
speech, given on January 20, 1961

CHAPTER 26

Our children's country

WHEN I STARTED THIS JOURNEY, I DID SO OUT OF concern for the country my children would inherit. As we grow older, the next generation of Americans will advance, and will eventually be in a position to purchase homes, raise families and assume leadership positions throughout our society.

In the meantime, our children are busy growing up, learning the alphabet and how to tie their shoes, and figuring out how life works overall. They rightfully aren't paying attention to the actions of those managing their country and what condition it will be in when they get old enough to need a job.

Just as we have a legal and moral obligation to care for our children as they grow up, don't we also have a duty to care for their assets until they're old enough to care for them themselves? Isn't it our fiduciary[1] duty to them—whether they are our children or grandchildren, or someone else's—to properly care for their country during their childhood? Until they're eighteen years old, they aren't allowed to vote regarding who should be on the management team that will make the decisions they'll inherit and have to live with when they grow up.

We certainly need to live our lives and take what happiness we can from our country. After all, it belongs to us, too. But shouldn't we also

---

[1] "Fiduciary" is defined by the Macmillan Dictionary as responsibility for taking care of money or property that belongs to someone else.

care for it in such a way as to leave it in excellent shape for those who will come after us?

There was a point when I was writing this book that I considered delivering all of this information—our government's perpetual overspending, the rapid increase and enormous size of our national debt, and what that might mean for the next generation's prosperity (or lack of it)—directly *to* that generation. I think kids in general are incredibly bright, and know much more than we give them credit for.

I thought it over. What if I spoke to kids in schools around the country about all the overspending their government has done, and the enormous debt it has left for them to deal with when they get older? What if I showed the third graders, who are eight years old now, that when they turn eighteen and have a chance to vote, it's estimated that their government will owe over $25 trillion, that it will be borrowing almost a trillion dollars a year to cover its overspending, and that it will be paying around the same amount in interest payments?[2] Shouldn't we let them know what management is doing that they'll inherit when they grow up?

My thinking was that the kids, armed with this information, could have a discussion about it with their parents (the current board members) over dinner at home, and that this might be the exact catalyst required to cause the change we need.

When I proposed this idea to people I knew, their reaction was decidedly negative. They didn't think it would be good to give such depressing information to kids, since it would surely upset them.

I understand this viewpoint. I certainly don't want to upset kids needlessly. And the information *is* upsetting—it upset me so much that I've dedicated a portion of my life to writing this book!

But does giving them factual information regarding their government's performance in running their country fall under the

---

[2] Edelberg, "CBO's Projection of Federal Interest Payments"; Congressional Budget Office, "Updated Budget Projections."

same category? Shouldn't we respect their right to know? And couldn't they, in speaking out, help pressure management into running their country better? Couldn't they encourage their parents and relatives to vote in a way that will ensure the financial stability of their country— so they actually have a fighting chance of getting a job, buying a home and supporting their family when they grow up?

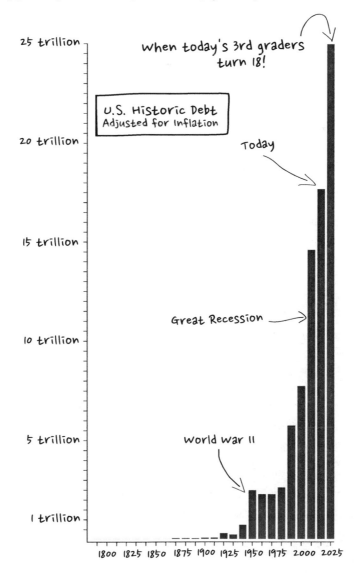

Sources: Data from Edelberg (2014); Sahr (2015); Bureau of Labor Statistics CPI Inflation Calculator.

If it's too uncomfortable for us as board members, or for those on the management team in Washington, to expose our children to the *truth* of what we're doing to their country, and what they'll have to live with for the rest of their lives, then isn't it obvious that we're doing something wrong, and that we need to change our ways?

Yes, this is a difficult topic to face up to. Yes, it seems impossible for us to stop our management team's constant overspending.

But face it today and do something about it we *must*, for if we don't, our debt will continue to skyrocket, interest rates will surely rise and we won't be able to make the payments we owe. And when that happens, we, along with our children and grandchildren, will potentially be faced with a global financial disaster of a magnitude never experienced before in history. At that point, it'll be too late to fix it. The time to shake up the system and force the change in government policy is *now*.

When you enter that voting booth in the next election and you're by yourself, you'll have a choice. You can select our country's management the same way you always have, or you can press the reset button with me and send *new* management to D.C. You can use your power however you choose, without anyone knowing what action you took. Regardless of how you vote, I hope you will do your job as a member of our country's board of directors and vote exactly the way *you* think is best for *your* country.

Down the line, I want to be able to look my kids—and someday, my grandkids—in the eye and tell them I did all I could to change the financially irresponsible habits of our government. I want to tell them that I did all I could to ensure that the country they inherited would be financially strong and independent. I want to tell them that I did all I could to give them the same chance at prosperity that my generation, and those that came before me, enjoyed.

Don't you?

"Any people anywhere, being inclined and having the power, have the right to rise up, and shake off the existing government, and form a new one that suits them better."

—Congressman Abraham Lincoln in a speech given on the floor of the House of Representatives on January 12, 1848

CHAPTER 27

Your Reason to Reset

WE'RE ALL DIFFERENT. WHAT I THINK NEEDS TO be done may not align with what you want. My complaint with the government may not be the same as yours. What I see as a national problem may not be a concern for you. And that's completely natural. We all have our own lives and points of view, and our government and its laws and policies will affect us all slightly differently.

The beauty of us all working together to reset our government—to vote everyone out and bring a fresh management team in—is that we don't all have to agree on the same reason for doing it.

If you're upset about an issue other than our national debt and overspending, then you can work in unison with everyone else who's also frustrated (for *their* own reasons) to send a very clear and powerful message to our elected leaders.

They need to listen to us; we're in charge.

———————————

"When the American people want a change
of Government—even when they merely
want 'new faces'—they can raise the old
electioneering battle cry of 'throw the rascals
out.'"

—President Franklin D. Roosevelt in a radio
address given to the American people from the
White House on October 5, 1944

———————————

CHAPTER 28

Share

I HOPE THAT, BY READING THIS BOOK, YOU'VE gained a new appreciation for the power of your vote. It's the *only* action we can take as citizens that has any binding power and legal effect on our government. In fact, it is the *absolute power* in our country—above the president, Congress, the Supreme Court and even our Constitution.

I encourage you to pass this information on to other members of our country's board of directors, because the power of pressing the reset button depends *entirely* on how many of us do it in the same election. We need to inform and encourage others to press it, too. Please feel free to post about it on Facebook, comment about it on Twitter and suggest that others get involved via other social networking sites.

You can also give them this book to read, or purchase more and hand them out to your contacts. If you own a business, you can give the book to your employees and make it available to your customers, or email them the link ResetOurGov.org so they can learn more.

In the end, if we get enough people working together by using the voting method laid out here, we'll have a new, more competent government and be on our way to a healthier country.

If you agree, *tell others.*

———————

"It is rather for us, the living, we here be dedicated to the great task remaining before us . . . that the nation, shall have a new birth of freedom, and that government of the people, by the people, for the people, shall not perish from the earth."

—President Abraham Lincoln in a speech given on November 19, 1863, to dedicate a national cemetery at the site of a bloody Civil War battle that had taken place five months earlier in Gettysburg, Pennsylvania

———————

For More Information

For more information about volunteering or making a donation, or to learn more about how you can help reset America, contact Reset Our Gov via our website, ResetOurGov.org. Reset Our Gov is a 501(c)(3) nonprofit corporation.

To contact Sean Burke, the author of this book and founder of Reset Our Gov, please email him at sburke@resetourgov.org.

Appendix

New to the process of voting, or living in a new area? Turn the page to learn your first steps to pressing the reset button.

How to Register to Vote

In every state but North Dakota, if you want to vote in an election, you'll need to register to vote. Most states require you to register ahead of the election. Some allow online registration, but most require you to mail in or drop off your information.

In order to vote in the United States, you have to be a citizen. Green cards and other non-citizen statuses don't qualify (fines, jail time and deportation can be the penalties for non-citizens claiming that they're citizens and voting.) You also need to be at least eighteen years old.

Other than these two primary requirements, each state can make its own voting eligibility rules (to a certain extent). So as you move forward with registering to vote, just ensure that you're eligible to vote in the area where you currently live. And if you move to a new county, you'll need to register again.

You can find voter registration information at your local post office, department of motor vehicles and most libraries.

The federal government has a website that provides voter registration information for every state in the country. They also provide a form you can fill out and the address you need to mail it to in your local area so that you become registered to vote. You can access the site at EAC.gov.

I've also listed links to voter registration information for all fifty states at ResetOurGov.org.

However you do it, I encourage you to register so you have the option of voting when there is an election.

How to vote

Voting on Election Day is very easy. Here are the three things you'll need to know:

WHERE TO VOTE: Since you currently can't vote online, you have to physically go to a designated location to place your vote. This is usually called a "polling place" or "polling station." "Polling" simply means "the act of voting."[1] So a "polling place" just means the place where you do your voting.

Before the election, your county will usually send you a sample ballot. A ballot is simply "the paper on which a vote is recorded."[2] The location where you can vote is usually listed on the outside of that ballot. Sometimes, after you've registered, your local government will mail you a voter registration card that will indicate your voting location on it, which is usually a local church, community center, school or other place.

Every county usually has a way for you to look online to find your polling place. Just search for your county plus the words "polling location" and you should see a link that will help you find the correct place to vote.

If all else fails, call your local county and ask where you should vote.

WHAT YOU WILL VOTE ON: As mentioned above, after you've registered to vote, you should receive a sample ballot in the mail prior

---

[1] Webster's New World Dictionary.

[2] Collins English Dictionary.

to the election. The sample ballot usually is an exact replica of what you'll receive when you get to your polling place to vote. This allows you to look over what you're going to vote on ahead of time, so you aren't surprised when you enter the voting booth. And, if you like, you can study the issues or candidates as much as you like beforehand.

HOW TO CAST YOUR VOTE: Okay, it's Election Day. You've already received your sample ballot, and you arrive at your polling place and walk in. In many polling places, you'll need to show some form of identification; in others, you won't. (A very good overview of these requirements can be found at NCSL.org.)

Once you receive your official voting ballot from those at the voting place, you'll go over to a designated place (usually a booth of some kind) where you will be able to mark your ballot in privacy. (Again, the way you vote is entirely up to you, and no one will know how you voted.)

Once in your booth, you will then open your ballot and simply follow the instructions on how to vote. In some places, you'll fill in circles by hand. Other voting places have mechanical devices that you'll use to vote. If you don't understand how to mark your choices, ask the election officials at your location for help.

In most places, if you don't want to vote for the candidates listed, you can also write in the name of someone else you'd like to represent you in that government position. Not every state allows this, and some require the write-in candidate to register prior to Election Day. Though it's a long shot, someone can potentially get elected using this method. Over the last hundred years, at least seven congressional candidates have won in this way.

When you're done voting, follow the instructions on your ballot about how to turn it in.

Once you've turned in your ballot, you're done. That's it. You've used your unique and tremendous power. Go on with the rest of your day, and feel good about fulfilling your duty.

Bibliography

Abraham Lincoln Association. "The Collected Works of Abraham Lincoln." Accessed February 20, 2015. http://quod.lib.umich.edu/l/lincoln.

Adams, John, and Charles Francis Adams. *The Works of John Adams, Second President of the United States.* Little, Brown, 1850.

American Heritage Dictionary. 5th ed. Dell, 2012. Also available at https://www.ahdictionary.com.

American Presidency Project. "Calvin Coolidge: Address Before the Daughters of the American Revolution, Washington D.C." Accessed February 20, 2015. http://www.presidency.ucsb.edu/ws/?pid=393.

———. "Franklin D. Roosevelt: 90—Address at Marietta, Ohio." Accessed February 20, 2015. http://www.presidency.ucsb.edu/ws/index.php?pid=15672.

———. "Franklin D. Roosevelt: 90—Radio Address from the White House." Accessed February 20, 2015. http://www.presidency.ucsb.edu/ws/?pid=16574.

———. "John F. Kennedy: 478—Remarks Intended for Delivery to the Texas Democratic State Committee in the Municipal Auditorium in Austin." Accessed February 20, 2015. http://www.presidency.ucsb.edu/ws/index.php?pid=9540&st=&st1=.

———. "Theodore Roosevelt: Fifth Annual Message." Accessed February 23, 2013. http://www.presidency.ucsb.edu/ws/?pid=29546.

Ancient Egypt Site. "History of Ancient Egypt." Last modified September 17, 2014. http://www.ancient-egypt.org/history/index.html.

Bartleby. "Respectfully Quoted: A Dictionary of Quotations. 1989." Accessed March 15, 2015. http://www.bartleby.com/73/1593.html.

Bertoni, Steven. "Billionaire Sheldon Adelson Says He Might Give $100M to Newt Gingrich or Other Republican." *Forbes,* February 21, 2012. http://www.forbes.com/sites/stevenbertoni/2012/02/21/billionaire-sheldon-adelson-says-he-might-give-100m-to-newt-gingrich-or-other-republican.

Bravin, Jess, and Colleen McCain Nelson. "Supreme Court Ends Overall Limit on Political Donations." *Wall Street Journal*, April 2, 2014. http://www.wsj.com/articles/SB10001424052 702303847804579477280434759494.

"The Budget and Economic Outlook: 2015 to 2025." Congressional Budget Office, January 26, 2015. https://www.cbo.gov/publication/49892.

Bui, Quoctrung. "Everyone the U.S. Government Owes Money To, In One Graph." National Public Radio, October 10, 2013. http://www.npr.org/blogs/money/2013/10/10/230944425/everyone-the-u-s-government-owes-money-to-in-one-graph.

Bureau of Labor Statistics CPI Inflation Calculator. Accessed September 9, 2015. http://www.bls.gov/data/inflation_calculator.htm.

Burns, Lawton R., John Cacciamani, James Clement, and Welman Aquino. "The Fall of the House of AHERF: The Allegheny Bankruptcy." Project HOPE, 2000. http://content.healthaffairs.org/content/19/1/7.full.pdf.

Burrows, Edwin G. "Patriots or Terrorists?" American Heritage Society, Fall 2008. http://www.americanheritage.com/content/patriots-or-terrorists?page=2.

"Chicago Voter Registration at Record Low." CBS News Chicago, February 13, 2012. http://chicago.cbslocal.com/2012/02/13/chicago-voter-registration-at-record-low.

Calmes, Jackie, and Megan Thee-Brenan. "Surveys of Voters Signal Dismay With Both Parties." New York Times, November 4, 2014. http://www.nytimes.com/2014/11/05/us/politics/surveys-of-voters-signal-dismay-with-both-parties.html?action=click&pgtype=Home page&module=span-abc-region&region=span-abc-region&WT.nav=span-abc-region&_r=2.

Carpenter, Francis. *Six Months at the White House with Abraham Lincoln*. White House Historical Association, 2008.

Choma, Russ. "Election 2012: The Big Picture Shows Record Cost of Winning a Seat in Congress." Center for Responsive Politics, June 19, 2013. http://www.opensecrets.org/news/2013/06/2012-overview.

City of Beverly Hills Study Session Action Minutes. Point 9. City of Beverly Hills, February 12, 2012. http://beverlyhills.granicus.com/MediaPlayer.php?view_id=2&clip_id=2611.

Collins English Dictionary. 9th ed. Collins, 2007. Also available at http://www.collinsdictionary.com/dictionary/english.

"Congressional Performance." Rasmussen Reports, February 20, 2015. http://www.rasmussenreports.com/public_content/politics/mood_of_america/congressional_performance.

"Congressional Performance." Rasmussen Reports, July 9, 2015. http://www.rasmussenreports.com/public_content/politics/mood_of_america/congressional_performance.

Constitution Society. "Thomas Jefferson, to Samuel Kercheval." Accessed February 20, 2015. http://www.constitution.org/tj/ltr/1816/ltr_18160712_kercheval.html.

"Democracy Index 2014." Economist Intelligence Unit, January 28, 2015. http://www.eiu.com/Handlers/WhitepaperHandler.ashx?fi=Democracy-index-2014.pdf&mode=wp&campaignid=Democracy0115.

"Department of Homeland Security Appropriations: FY2014 Overview and Summary." Congressional Research Service, March 11, 2014. https://www.fas.org/sgp/crs/homesec/R43193.pdf.

Edelberg, Wendy. "CBO's Projection of Federal Interest Payments." Congressional Budget Office, September 3, 2014. https://www.cbo.gov/publication/45684.

Encyclopedia Britannica. "Ancient Greek Civilization." Last modified January 22, 2015. http://www.britannica.com/EBchecked/topic/244231/ancient-Greek-civilization.

———. "Ancient Rome." Last modified July 17, 2014. http://www.britannica.com/EBchecked/topic/507905/ancient-Rome.

———. "British Empire." Last modified May 1, 2014. http://www.britannica.com/EBchecked/topic/80013/British-Empire.

———. "Ostracism." Last modified June 16, 2013. http://www.britannica.com/EBchecked/topic/434423/ostracism.

Farm Credit Administration. "History of FCA and the FCS." Last modified September 22, 2014. http://www.fca.gov/about/history/historyFCA_FCS.html.

"FEC Summarizes Campaign Activity of the 2011-2012 Election Cycle." Federal Election Commission, March 27, 2014. http://www.fec.gov/press/press2013/20130419_2012-24m-Summary.shtml.

"The Federal Education Budget." New America Foundation, April 30, 2014. http://febp.newamerica.net/background-analysis/education-federal-budget.

The Federalist Papers Project. "John Adams Quotes." Accessed February 23, 2015. http://www.thefederalistpapers.org/founders/john-adams.

"53% Think Neither Political Party Represents the American People." Rasmussen Reports, April 24, 2014. http://www.rasmussenreports.com/public_content/politics/general_politics/april_2014/53_think_neither_political_party_represents_the_american_people.

Gettysburg Foundation. "Copies of the Gettysburg Address." Accessed February 20, 2015. http://www.gettysburgfoundation.org/41.

HerbertHoover.org. "Herbert Hoover." Accessed February 23, 2015. http://www.herberthoover.org/.

Janison, Dan. "Voter Turnout Disappointing in Tuesday's Elections." Newsday, November 11, 2013. http://www.newsday.com/columnists/dan-janison/voter-turnout-disappointing-in-tuesday-s-elections-1.6413164.

John F. Kennedy Presidential Library and Museum. "John F. Kennedy Quotations." Accessed February 20, 2015. http://www.jfklibrary.org/Research/Research-Aids/Ready-Reference/JFK-Quotations.aspx.

————. "John F. Kennedy Quotations: President Kennedy's Inaugural Address, January 20, 1961." Accessed February 20, 2015. http://www.jfklibrary.org/Research/Research-Aids/Ready-Reference/JFK-Quotations/Inaugural-Address.aspx.

Joint Congressional Committee on Inaugural Ceremonies. "Address by John Quincy Adams, 1825." Accessed February 20, 2015. http://www.inaugural.senate.gov/swearing-in/address/address-by-john-quincy-adams-1825.

Kennedy, John F. Profiles in Courage. HarperCollins Publishers, 2006.

Lapsley, Arthur Brooks, ed. The Papers and Writings of Abraham Lincoln, Complete Constitutional Edition. Project Gutenberg, 2012. E-book edition. http://www.gutenberg.org/files/3253/3253-h/3253-h.htm.

Levenson, Michael. "After Her Record Haul, Warren Slips Into Red." Boston Globe, December 5, 2012. http://www.bostonglobe.com/news/politics/2012/12/05/elizabeth-warren-ended-senate-campaign-debt-despite-record-fund-raising/ShWe5K7KzUiVnFHiIxkX5H/story.html.

Library of Congress. "The Articles of Confederation." Accessed February 20, 2015. http://www.loc.gov/rr/program/bib/ourdocs/articles.html.

————. "The Thomas Jefferson Papers Series 1. General Correspondence." Accessed February 20, 2015. http://memory.loc.gov/cgi-bin/ampage?collId=mtj1&fileName=mtj1page052. db&recNum=402.

Macmillan Dictionary for Students. Ltd. Pan Macmillan, 1984.

MacNevin, Suzanne. "The Spanish Inquisition: Killing Non-Christians for the Mother Church." Lilith Gallery of Toronto, 2010. http://www.lilithgallery.com/library/christian/The_ Spanish_Inquisition.html.

Merriam-Webster Dictionary. Merriam-Webster Mass Market, 2004. Also available at http:// www.merriam-webster.com.

NASA. "NASA FY 2016 Budget Request." Accessed September 12, 2015. http://www.nasa. gov/sites/default/files/files/Agency_Fact_Sheet_FY_2016.pdf.

National Archives. "From George Washington to Bushrod Washington, 9 November 1787." Accessed February 20, 2015. http://founders.archives.gov/GEWN-04-05-02-0388.

————. "From George Washington to Charles Mynn Thruston, 10 August 1794." Accessed February 20, 2015. http://founders.archives.gov/documents/Washington/05-16-02-0376.

————. "From John Adams to Boston Patriot, 4 August 1809." Accessed February 20, 2015. http://founders.archives.gov/documents/Adams/99-02-02-5405.

————. "New York Ratifying Convention. Remarks (Francis Childs's Version), [27 June 1788]." Accessed February 20, 2015. http://founders.archives.gov/documents/ Hamilton/01-05-02-0012-0034.

————. "Teaching with Documents: An Act of Courage, the Arrest Records of Rosa Parks." Accessed February 2, 2015. http://www.archives.gov/education/lessons/rosa-parks.

————. "Thomas Jefferson to Albert Gallatin, 11 October 1809." Accessed February 20, 2015. http://founders.archives.gov/documents/Jefferson/03-01-02-0471.

————. "Thomas Jefferson to the Republicans of Washington County, Maryland, 31 March 1809." Accessed February 20, 2015. http://founders.archives.gov/documents/ Jefferson/03-01-02-0088.

————. "To Alexander Hamilton from George Washington, 28 August 1788." Accessed February 20, 2015. http://founders.archives.gov/documents/Hamilton/01-05-02-0025.

National Endowment for the Humanities. "Lesson 1: The Road to the Constitutional Convention." Accessed February 20, 2015. http://edsitement.neh.gov/lesson-plan/road-constitutional-convention.

New America. "Federal Education Budget Overview." Last modified July 8, 2015. http://atlas.newamerica.org/education-federal-budget.

New World Encyclopedia. "Theodore Roosevelt." Last modified February 4, 2012. http://www.newworldencyclopedia.org/entry/Theodore_Roosevelt.

Oxford English Dictionary. 7th ed. Oxford University Press, 2013. Also available at http://www.oed.com.

Peckham, Howard H., ed. *The Toll of Independence: Engagements and Battle Casualties of the American Revolution.* University of Chicago Press, 1974.

"Right Direction or Wrong Track." Rasmussen Reports, January 28, 2015. http://www.rasmussenreports.com/public_content/politics/mood_of_america/right_direction_or_wrong_track.

Rosiak, Luke. "Congressional Staffers, Public Shortchanged by High Turnover, Low Pay." Washington Times, June 6, 2012. http://www.washingtontimes.com/news/2012/jun/6/congressional-staffers-public-shortchanged-by-high/?page=all.

Sahr, Robert C. "Consumer Price Index (CPI) Conversion Factors for Years 1774 to Estimated 2025 to Convert to Dollars of 2014." Last modified February 5, 2015. http://liberalarts.oregonstate.edu/sites/liberalarts.oregonstate.edu/files/polisci/faculty-research/sahr/inflation-conversion/pdf/cv2014.pdf.

Schweizer, Peter. *Extortion: How Politicians Extract Your Money, Buy Votes, and Line Their Own Pockets.* Houghton Mifflin Harcourt Trade, 2013.

Stone, Peter H. "Sheldon Adelson Spent Far More On Campaign Than Previously Known." *Huffington Post,* December 3, 2012. http://www.huffingtonpost.com/2012/12/03/sheldon-adelson-2012-election_n_2223589.html.

Texas Secretary of State. "Turnout and Voter Registration Figures (1970–Current)." Accessed February 2, 2015. http://www.sos.state.tx.us/elections/historical/70-92.shtml.

Treasury Direct. "The Debt to the Penny and Who Holds It." Last modified January 30, 2015. http://www.treasurydirect.gov/NP/debt/current.

United States Department of Veterans Affairs. "Expenditures." Last Modified May 29, 2015. http://www.va.gov/vetdata/Expenditures.asp.

United States Election Project. "2014 November General Election Turnout Rates." Last modified December 30, 2014. http://www.electproject.org/2014g.

"Updated Budget Projections: 2015 to 2025." Congressional Budget Office, March 9, 2015. https://www.cbo.gov/publication/49973.

"Voters Question Whether Either Major Party Has A Plan for the Future." Rasmussen Reports, October 9, 2014. http://www.rasmussenreports.com/public_content/politics/general_politics/october_2014/voters_question_whether_either_major_party_has_a_plan_for_the_future.

Webster's New World Dictionary. 5th ed. Webster's New World, 2014.

Welsh, Ben. "L.A. Mayoral Runoff Another Low Mark in Voter Turnout: 23.3%." Los Angeles Times, June 11, 2013. http://www.latimes.com/local/la-me-final-la-vote-20130611-story.html.

White House Office of Management and Budget. "Historical Tables." Accessed February 2, 2015. http://www.whitehouse.gov/omb/budget/Historicals.

Wikipedia. "List of Sovereign States by Date of Formation." Last modified February 19, 2015. http://en.wikipedia.org/wiki/List_of_sovereign_states_by_date_of_formation.

Wikisource. "Life and Works of Abraham Lincoln/Volume 3/Arraignment of President Polk for War Against Mexico." Last modified January 10, 2011. http://en.wikisource.org/wiki/Life_and_Works_of_Abraham_Lincoln/Volume_3/Arraignment_of_President_Polk_for_War_Against_Mexico#128.

Yale Law School Lillian Goldman Law Library. "First Inaugural Address of Abraham Lincoln." The Avalon Project. Accessed February 20, 2015. http://www.loc.gov/teachers/newsevents/events/lincoln/pdf/avalonFirst.pdf.

———. "Opinion on the French Treaties." The Avalon Project. Accessed February 20, 2015. http://avalon.law.yale.edu/18th_century/jeffop2.asp.

———. "Washington's Farewell Address 1796." The Avalon Project. Accessed February 23, 2015. http://avalon.law.yale.edu/18th_century/washing.asp.

Zahniser, David. "Panel Wants L.A. to Look at Using Prizes to Boost Voter Turnout." Los Angeles Times, August 14, 2014. http://www.latimes.com/local/lanow/la-me-ln-panel-prizes-voters-20140814-story.html.